Hygge Harmony

Embracing Coziness in Everyday Life

Emma Christensen

Table of Contents

INTRODUCTION

Hygge, a Danish term that means "warmth, comfort, and a sense of belonging," offers a welcome counterbalance to a world that is frequently hectic, disorganized, and disengaged. The book "Hygge Harmony: Embracing Coziness in Everyday Life" provides guidance on comprehending and incorporating this lovely concept into your daily life. This book will walk you through the core ideas of Hygge, teaching you how to make comfortable spaces, develop deep connections, and discover happiness in the little things in life.

More than just a fad in lifestyle, hygge (pronounced "hoo-ga") is a deeply embedded cultural practice in Denmark that places a strong emphasis on comfort, satisfaction, and well-being. Since the term itself contains a wide range of emotions and experiences, it is challenging to translate precisely into English. It's a sensation of coziness and warmth, a shared moment of tranquility, and a mental condition in which contentment thrives. The coziness of a wool blanket, the soft glow of a candle, and laughing with loved ones over a home-cooked dinner are all examples of hygge. It's an experience that perfectly encapsulates what it means to be entirely at home.

Hygge's accessibility and simplicity are its main features. Hygge is a lifestyle philosophy that anybody, anywhere, can adopt, unlike other trends that could be needed for significant financial or lifestyle changes. It encourages you to value the little things and discover joy in ordinary situations rather than requiring you to adhere to rigid standards or support a specific brand. This book seeks to teach you how to apply Hygge to your life, bringing balance and harmony that may elevate the ordinary to the remarkable.

You will be guided through many facets of Hygge in the ensuing chapters, beginning with an examination of its foundations and tenets. You will discover the cultural and historical background that molded Hygge into its current form and how it spread to other parts of the world, not only Denmark. We'll explore the essential Hygge principles—coziness, community, and mindfulness—and how they can improve your mental and emotional health.

One of the easiest ways to live this idea is to create a Hygge atmosphere at home. You'll learn how to use lighting, textures, and colors to decorate your living area in a way that encourages coziness and comfort. We'll talk about how important it is to simplify and tidy your house in order to make it seem calm and inviting. Another essential component of Hygge is integrating nature into your living area. No matter the season, there are ideas for doing this.

Hygge is a concept that you can enjoy year-round in a variety of contexts and not just in your house. From the coziness of a summertime picnic beneath the stars to the warmth of a crackling fire in winter, every season presents its own possibilities to embrace Hygge. This book will walk you through seasonal Hygge activities so you can discover methods to be comfortable and happy regardless of the weather.

Hygge has the power to change ordinary tasks. You will discover how to bring warmth and delight into everyday moments through activities like crafting and hobbies, as well as mindful eating and drinking. Another critical component of hygiene is self-care, and this book will provide you with techniques and routines to enhance your wellbeing.

Connections are the core of Hygge. A sense of contentment and belonging can only be attained by forging close bonds with friends, family, and neighbors.

This book will look at how to create these bonds via meaningful exchanges and shared experiences.

Hygge can also be used in the workplace to help you establish a harmonious and rewarding atmosphere. Using Hygge principles can improve your well-being and productivity whether you work in an office or from home.

A Hygge lifestyle is centered around mindfulness and personal development. This book will help you develop a grateful attitude, realistic goals, and an optimistic outlook. Sustainable living techniques will teach you how to live more in harmony with nature, while hygge-inspired travel advice will assist you in organizing vacations that prioritize leisure and enjoyment.

It's critical to balance technology in the digital age with the concepts of Hygge. There are techniques for controlling screen time, utilizing technology sensibly, and establishing digital balance in your life.

Your all-inclusive guide to incorporating the magic of hygge into every aspect of your life is "Hygge Harmony: Embracing Coziness in Everyday Life." This book will encourage you to design a life that is warm, joyful, and connected, regardless of whether you are unfamiliar with the idea or seeking to expand your practice. So take a warm blanket and a candle, and let's start this adventure to learn about the art of living well through the concept of hygge.

CHAPTER I

Understanding Hygge

Exploring the Danish concept of Hygge

Pronounce it "hoo-ga," the Danish concept of Hygge has gained popularity throughout the world as a way to foster contentment, coziness, and well-being in daily life. Originally from Denmark, the idea of Hygge is a distinct way of living that prioritizes comfort, joy, and community. This section explores how the Hygge concept may turn ordinary moments into remarkable experiences and promote a life of warmth and harmony by delving into its history, tenets, and real-world applications.

Hygge's origins can be found in Old Norse, where the word "hugga" denoted consolation or solace. This idea developed over centuries into the contemporary Danish practice of hygiene, which includes a wide variety of sensations and experiences associated with comfort and wellbeing. Denmark has adopted Hygge as a pillar of its culture and is frequently named one of the happiest nations in the world. The country's interior design, architecture, social rituals, and even official policy have all been impacted by this national embrace of Hygge, which has improved the general happiness and well-being of its people.

Hygge is essentially about finding contentment and comfort in the here and now. It promotes awareness and enjoyment of life's little pleasures, like the comfort of a warm blanket, the enchanting glimmer of a candle, or the excitement of dining with close friends and family. Hygge is about finding beauty and contentment in the commonplace, not about luxury or financial wealth. For many who are trying to get away from the stresses and diversions of contemporary life, this emphasis on mindfulness and simplicity is significant.

Making a cozy and welcoming environment is one of the core tenets of hygiene. This can be accomplished by carefully planning the interior to give comfort and coziness first priority. Natural materials, calm-promoting minimalist décor, and gentle lighting are standard features of Danish homes. A fundamental component of Hygge, candles provide a gentle, flickering light that fosters a tranquil atmosphere. In a similar vein, adding warmth and texture to the living area through the use of natural materials like stone, wool, and wood improves the room's overall comfort level.

The value of being together is another essential component of hygiene. Hygge promotes deepening relationships via meaningful interactions and shared experiences with friends, family, and neighbors. At a family meal, a casual get-together with friends, or a community function, Hygge stresses the need to be totally present and involved with people around us. Relationships are essential for mental health because they provide a sense of support and belonging.

The Hygge lifestyle transcends the boundaries of the house and is available all year round. Every season presents different chances to adopt a hygge lifestyle. Hygge is best experienced in the wintertime among the coziness of a hot beverage, the warmth of a crackling fire, and the delight of festive get-togethers. With the rebirth of nature that spring offers, people can enjoy being outside and watching flowers bloom. Autumn's brilliant foliage and crisp air make it the ideal time of year to curl up with a good book and have a hearty dinner, while summer's long days and warm weather are suitable for picnics, beach outings, and evening barbecues.

Another method to reap the benefits of Hygge is to incorporate it into daily tasks. For example, mindful drinking and eating can turn an essential meal into a Hygge encounter. This entails enjoying the companionship of those you dine with, savoring each bite, and appreciating the flavors and textures. Hygge also includes relaxing and having fun with crafts and pastimes. Crafts like knitting, painting, gardening, and baking promote creativity and a sense of achievement, which enhance happiness and well-being in general.

A key element of hygiene is self-care. Living a healthy and meaningful life requires prioritizing one's well-being and taking the time to care for oneself. Self-care activities that are influenced by the hygge lifestyle could involve doing yoga, reading a good book, having a long bath, or just pausing for some peaceful thought. These pursuits offer a chance to refuel and establish a connection with oneself, promoting a feeling of inner serenity and tranquility.

Additionally, hygiene has a significant effect on mental wellness. Stress and anxiety can be lessened by putting an emphasis on connection, mindfulness, and simplicity. Hygge promotes a good attitude in life by encouraging mindfulness and an appreciation of the little things in life. The concept of Hygge fosters a community of support and solid social ties to build emotional resilience. For one's general wellbeing and mental health, this sense of security and belonging is crucial.

In the workplace, implementing the concepts of Hygge can lead to increased productivity and job happiness. Whether at home or at an office, setting up a comfortable and practical workspace can enhance focus and creativity. Personal touches like plants or photographs, cozy chairs, and gentle lighting can all contribute to a more welcoming work atmosphere. It's also critical to keep a healthy work-life balance. In the long run, increased productivity and job happiness might result from hygiene's encouragement of setting boundaries and taking regular breaks to relax and recharge.

A hygge mindset when traveling facilitates more laid-back and pleasurable encounters. Whether taking a staycation or traveling to new places, applying the concepts of Hygge can improve the trip experience. This could entail selecting cozy and comfortable lodging, organizing leisurely and socially engaging activities, and appreciating the cuisine and culture of the area. Traveling with an emphasis on comfort and wellbeing allows one to make lifelong memories and significant experiences.

Another crucial component of Hygge is sustainability. This way of thinking promotes making decisions that will support a sustainable future and living in balance with the environment. This could entail implementing eco-friendly habits like cutting back on waste, buying natural and organic products, and patronizing ethical and locally owned companies. One can improve their own well-being and contribute to the health of the earth by making conscious and sustainable decisions.

It's crucial to strike a balance between technology and Hygge in the digital age. Even though technology has many advantages, it can also be distracting and stressful. Hygge promotes the thoughtful use of technology, establishing tech-free zones or periods of time to concentrate on leisure and hygiene. This may be establishing limits on screen time, participating in tech-free events like dinners and get-togethers, and looking for screen-free hobbies. An individual can lead a more contented and balanced existence by practicing mindful technology management.

Hygge's enormous appeal indicates a desire for a more contented and balanced lifestyle. Hygge provides a route to increased pleasure and well-being for individuals all over the world who are trying to get away from the stresses and diversions of contemporary life. By adopting the tenets of Hygge, one can create a life that is cozy, harmonious, and full of moments of delight and contentment out of ordinary experiences.

To sum up, the Danish idea of hygge offers a helpful framework for building a cozy, contented, and happy life. Hygge promotes a more contented and balanced way of living by emphasizing the small things in life, building solid connections, and practicing mindfulness. Hygge offers a plethora of options to improve happiness and well-being, whether through intentional interior design, seasonal activities, or daily habits. Embracing Hygge can help us find joy and harmony in everyday moments as we manage the difficulties and complexities of modern life, leading to a life rich in coziness and connection.

Historical context and cultural significance

The ability of Hygge, a Danish notion that encompasses coziness, comfort, and a feeling of well-being, to improve everyday living has attracted interest from all around the world. It is essential to comprehend the cultural significance and historical background of Hygge in order to truly appreciate it. The history of Hygge, how it has changed over time, and how it has impacted Danish culture and society are all explored in this section. We can better understand why Hygge appeals to people in Denmark and around the world by examining these elements.

"Hygge" is a Norwegian word that means "well-being." It first surfaced in 18th-century Danish literature and has since developed into a fundamental facet of Danish society. The severe weather and difficult living circumstances of Scandinavia are the origins of Hygge. Due to its long, gloomy winters and cool, rainy weather, Denmark had to prioritize making their homes cozy and comfortable. In order to improve life's quality regardless of the outside surroundings, the concept of Hygge was developed in response to this demand for indoor warmth.

Hygge was first mostly connected to the home and family life. The Danish people started to emphasize the importance of designing cozy and welcoming living areas. The greater European tendency of the 17th and 18th centuries, in which the home and family life became fundamental to social and cultural identity, can be connected to this emphasis on domesticity. However, the terrible weather in Denmark made it necessary to spend a significant amount of time indoors, which increased this trend. Homes were built with features like fireplaces, limited windows, and thick walls to optimize warmth and comfort. Natural elements like wool and wood were used, which increased the feeling of coziness and warmth.

Hygge's cultural relevance was further cemented in the 19th century during the Industrial Revolution. Denmark saw a change from rural to urban existence as it, along with many other nations, rapidly industrialized. The people experienced stress and a sense of displacement as a result of the substantial social and economic changes brought about by this shift. Hygge evolved as a way to deal with these shifts, offering comfort and stability in a world that was changing quickly. The house continued to be a haven, a place where people could escape the mayhem and find comfort in the little things in life.

Hygge was also popularized by the Danish folk high school movement, which had its start in the middle of the 19th century. The significance of community, personal growth, and cultural legacy were stressed in these schools. They promoted a sense of community and togetherness, which are essential elements of Hygge. The movement inspired Danes to enjoy life on a daily basis and to value their cultural customs. The principles of Hygge were reaffirmed and further integrated into the Danish way of life by means of this cultural education.

The two World Wars that occurred in the 20th century had a lasting impression on Denmark and solidified the idea of Hygge. In these turbulent times, hygiene becomes an essential coping strategy. In the middle of the uncertainty, the emphasis on establishing a warm and inviting home atmosphere offered a sense of stability and regularity. Families came together to comfort one another, highlighting the value of unity and solidarity amongst one another. Hygge provided a means of preserving one's sense of wellbeing in the face of chaos outside.

Denmark saw tremendous social and economic changes following World War II. The establishment of the welfare state raised living standards and increased social security. Hygge became more than merely a reaction to outside adversity as a result of these changes. It developed into a deliberate way of living that reflected the more significant social goals of equality, community, and well-being. The welfare state's goals of ensuring the welfare of all residents were in line with the emphasis on establishing a cozy and welcoming home environment.

Numerous facets of daily life in modern Denmark demonstrate the cultural significance of Hygge. Danish design, which is well-known for its practicality and simplicity, frequently uses Hygge components. Warmth and comfort are emphasized in the design of furniture and home décor, which places a focus on natural materials, subdued lighting, and minimalist aesthetics. The greater cultural emphasis put on creating hospitable and harmonious living places is reflected in this design philosophy.

Hygge is also very important for community life and social connections. Danes place a high value on spending time with their loved ones, and they frequently get together for holidays, feasts, and informal get-togethers. These get-togethers are known for their laid-back, comfortable vibe, with an emphasis on savoring the present moment and each other's company. Hygge is embodied in the custom of "faellesspisning," or communal dining, which emphasizes the value of community and shared experiences.

Hygge has cultural relevance outside of the office as well. Danish workplace culture places a strong emphasis on work-life balance and values social relationships and individual wellbeing. Incorporating features of Hygge, workplaces are frequently intended to be cozy and friendly, fostering a happy and productive attitude. Policies pertaining to parental leave, paid time off, and flexible work schedules are indicative of society's overarching commitment to guaranteeing a good standard of living for all individuals.

In Denmark, Hygge has also made an appearance in public areas and urban design. The welcoming and inclusive designs of parks, cafes, and community centers promote social interaction and a feeling of community. Hygge is frequently incorporated into public gatherings and festivals, offering chances for people to mingle and celebrate in a warm and inviting setting. The emphasis on establishing Hygge in public areas is a reflection of the greater cultural importance ascribed to social cohesion and community.

The rising demand for a more contented and balanced lifestyle is what's behind Hygge's recent global appeal. Hygge provides a route to increased pleasure and well-being for individuals all over the world who are trying to get away from the stresses and diversions of contemporary life. The Danish idea of Hygge has gained international traction thanks to the proliferation of books, sections, and social media sections about it. The global fascination with Hygge underscores a shared desire for coziness, companionship, and satisfaction.

In summary, the cultural relevance and historical background of Hygge point to a firmly rooted and dynamic tradition that has influenced Danish culture for many years. Hygge has offered consolation, stability, and a sense of well-being since its inception as a reaction to inclement weather and difficult living circumstances. It has also played a part in helping people adjust to social and economic changes. Hygge still shapes public places, workplace culture, social interactions, and design in modern-day Denmark, reflecting the more significant cultural principles of equality, community, and quality of life. Hygge's appeal to people all around the world highlights its relevance to everyone, providing a timeless and approachable way to improve daily life.

How Hygge became popular worldwide

The Danish notion of Hygge, which embodies coziness, comfort, and a feeling of well-being, has evolved from a regional custom to a worldwide phenomenon. Numerous causes, including the growing importance of mental wellness, the impact of globalization, and the increasing focus on lifestyle trends that encourage serenity and simplicity, have contributed to its global growth in popularity. This section delves into the complex process of how Hygge spread over the world, looking at its history, the media's role, the impact of cultural changes, and its incorporation into many facets of living outside of Denmark.

The Danish word "hygge," pronounced "hoo-ga," comes from the Old Norse word "hugga," which meant to reassure or soothe. It was first used in the 18th century. It has long been an essential component of Danish culture, reflecting the nation's focus on social interaction, simplicity, and well-being. The long, gloomy winters and chilly climate of Denmark have historically necessitated a concentration on providing warmth and comfort indoors. Hygge, a way of living focused on savoring life's small pleasures—whether through food, drink, company, or alone time—evolved from this environmental necessity.

The mid-2010s saw a lot of societal and technical development, which is when Hygge first came into its own on a global scale. Digital platforms and social media's introduction were critical to this process. Sharing and enjoying photos and tales inspired by Hygge has taken off on social media platforms like Instagram, Pinterest, and lifestyle blogs. These channels' emphasis on visuals made it possible to effectively present the aesthetic elements of Hygge—like cozy rooms, candlelit dinners, and intimate gatherings—to a worldwide audience.

Publications and books also played a significant role in the global diffusion of the Hygge concept. "The Little Book of Hygge: Danish Secrets to Happy Living" by Meik Wiking, which was released in 2016, is among the most important publications. The CEO of the Happiness Research Institute in Copenhagen, Wiking, offered a clear and exciting explanation of Hygge, highlighting its capacity to improve wellbeing. His book was translated into several languages and became a worldwide success, igniting a global movement of interest in Hygge.

Hygge's surge in popularity occurred at the same time as a more general societal movement towards mental health, mindfulness, and a need for simplicity in a fast-paced environment. Growing awareness of the mental health problem and rising rates of anxiety, despair, and burnout—especially in Western societies—was evident by the mid-2010s. People were looking for ways to offset the disconnect and stress that come with living in the modern world. Hygge provided an enticing counterbalance to these stresses with its emphasis on slowing down, savoring the present, and creating meaningful connections.

The spread of Hygge was significantly aided by globalization as well. Global interconnectedness increased the frequency of cultural exchanges, which promoted a heightened awareness and acceptance of global behaviors. Denmark's standing as one of the happiest nations in the world attracted interest in its customs and way of life. People from other nations started to investigate how they could apply this idea to their own lives as H hygge became a vital component of the Danish way of life.

Hygge's versatility and accessibility are what make it so appealing. Hygge places a strong emphasis on appreciating small, everyday joys, in contrast to other lifestyle trends that could be needed for a large financial outlay or drastic lifestyle adjustments. It promotes cooking delicious meals, setting up a warm environment at home, and spending time with close friends and family. These are habits that everyone may follow, no matter where they live or their financial situation.

Beyond Denmark, Hygge has been incorporated into a number of spheres of life, such as wellness, gastronomy, fashion, and home décor. In the world of interior design, cozy, welcoming rooms are often associated with décor that draws inspiration from Hygge. Hygge's signature elements—the use of natural materials, gentle lighting, and cozy furnishings—have impacted international design trends. Retailers and businesses worldwide have benefited from this by marketing goods that claim to instill a hygienic feeling in their consumers' homes.

Hygge is credited with starting a fashion trend in which soft, comfy clothes are worn. The Hygge concept of coziness and warmth is reflected in the fashion for oversized sweaters, plush fabrics, and layering. This fashion emphasizes ease and relaxation over formality and confinement in clothing, not only for physical comfort but also to promote overall wellbeing.

Hygge has also caught on in the culinary realm, where comfort food and group eating are prioritized. Cookbooks and food blogs with an Hygge aesthetic have proliferated, featuring hearty, nourishing, and sharing-friendly dishes. One of the most iconic Hygge experiences is cooking and dining with loved ones, which emphasizes the value of community and connection.

Hygge-inspired wellness practices have become popular, encouraging pursuits that enhance mental and emotional well. These include self-care regimens that put an emphasis on rest and self-compassion, as well as mindfulness exercises like yoga and meditation. The holistic Hygge approach to wellbeing emphasizes a balanced and contented lifestyle while acknowledging the relationship between the mind, body, and spirit.

Hygge's global appeal has been aided by commercialization, but it has also spurred discussions concerning its appropriateness and genuineness. Some detractors contend that Hygge's monetization distorts its genuine meaning by turning a cultural custom into a commercial trend. They stress that hygiene is a deeply ingrained cultural practice that transcends commercial items and warn against reducing it to a collection of consumer goods. Notwithstanding these reservations, there is no denying that the popularity of Hygge has highlighted the importance of conscious living and small pleasures.

Hygge's widespread appeal has sparked similar lifestyle movements with distinct cultural twists in various nations. For instance, the Swedish idea of "Lagom," which translates to "just the right amount," places a strong emphasis on moderation and balance in all facets of life. The concept of "Ikigai," or "reason for being," is central to the Japanese practice of seeking fulfillment and meaning in life. Though different from Hygge, these ideas are similar in that they emphasize purposeful and thoughtful living as a means of fostering well-being.

In conclusion, a variety of variables, such as the impact of social media, the release of easily accessible books, societal movements toward mindfulness and mental wellness, and the results of globalization, have contributed to the global rise of the Hygge trend. Hygge's focus on coziness, comfort, and connection appeals to people all across the world and provides a straightforward yet effective means of improving daily living. Hygge reminds us of the enduring worth of small pleasures and the significance of promoting a sense of well-being and connection in our lives as it continues to inspire and impact all elements of world society.

CHAPTER II

Creating a Hygge Environment at Home

Key elements of Hygge décor (lighting, textures, colors)
Hygge, a Danish notion pronounced "hoo-gah," conjures up feelings of coziness, comfort, and happiness. It's a lifestyle that stresses the value of creating a cozy and welcoming environment rather than merely a design fad. The emphasis of Hygge design is on coziness, warmth, and wellbeing. Essential components of Hygge décor are colors, textures, and lighting, each of which is essential to creating the right atmosphere. This section explores these components and their roles in enhancing the Hygge experience as a whole.

Maybe the most critical component of Hygge décor is lighting. Lighting in the Danish way of life is more than just lighting a room; it's about establishing a mood that encourages intimacy and relaxation. Denmark's long, dark winters have made people appreciate cozy, delicate lighting that stands in stark contrast to the outer world. A variety of lighting fixtures, such as low-wattage bulbs, candles, and fairy lights, are employed to accomplish this.

An essential element of Hygge décor is candles. They give off a gentle, flickering light that makes any space feel cozier and warmer. Candlelight's organic, cozy radiance is ideal for establishing a comfortable and welcoming ambiance. Danes frequently use a lot of candles, scattering them on dining tables, windowsills, and even toilets. Candlelight adds a soft glow that can soothe and comfort people by creating a more peaceful and inviting atmosphere.

Another common lighting choice in Hygge décor is fairy lights, often known as string lights. These delicate lights give an area a fanciful, mystical feel. To create a delicate, glittering glow, they can be wrapped around plants, hung along walls, or draped over furniture. Living rooms and bedrooms feel more intimate and magical when lit with fairy lights, which are especially good at doing so.

Another requirement for Hygge lighting is low-wattage lightbulbs. Bright, harsh lighting can be distracting and work against the intention of fostering a calm atmosphere. Warm, gentle lighting is preferred instead.

Low-wattage light bulbs produce a soft light that is comfortable for the eyes and promotes a cozy and serene environment. Additionally well-liked are lamps with dimmers, which enable varying lighting settings to accommodate various activities and moods.

Textures, along with lighting, are essential components of Hygge décor. The way materials feel on the touch scale can have a significant impact on how a room feels overall. Hygge places a strong emphasis on the use of cozy, inviting textures that are warm and inviting to the touch.

Wool is one of the most popular textures in Hygge décor. Rugs, throws, and blankets made of wool are frequently used to make a room feel cozy and warm. Wool's velvety, cozy texture is ideal for curling up on a chilly day. Particularly, handmade, rustic charm is added by woolen goods that are knitted or woven, which elevates the Hygge ambiance.

Another familiar texture in Hygge décor is faux fur. Throws and pillows with faux fur give the space an opulent, cozy vibe. The fluffy, soft texture adds another degree of coziness and is quite appealing. Items with faux fur are frequently arranged on chairs or draped over couches to create comfortable spaces for unwinding.

Wood is a crucial component in Hygge design and is valued for its organic, natural texture. Wooden accessories, flooring, and furniture give a room a feeling of coziness and solidity. The wood's grain and texture bring a bit of the outdoors in, encouraging a connection to nature—a vital component of the Hygge lifestyle. Light-colored woods are trendy because they can add brightness to a space without sacrificing coziness, like oak and pine.

Another essential element of Hygge décor is soft textiles like linen and cotton. These materials are perfect for upholstery, curtains, and beds since they are cozy and breathable. The natural fibers of linen and cotton give a room a breezy, light quality that makes it feel comfortable and welcoming. Layering various textiles improves the tactile feel and provides the décor with depth, such as when cotton sheets are layered over woolen blankets.

Hygge décor uses carefully selected colors to produce a calming and relaxing atmosphere. Typically, the color scheme consists of muted, neutral tones that promote tranquility and harmony. The simplicity and beauty of the natural world are reflected in these colors, which were inspired by nature and the Scandinavian countryside.

In Hygge's interior design, whites, and off-whites are frequently utilized to create a light and airy ambiance. These hues reflect light, creating an air of openness and coziness in rooms. White walls offer a simple, impartial background that makes other components, such as textures and accessories, pop. Off-white colors like cream or ivory give the color scheme a hint of warmth and keep the room from appearing overly clinical or austere.

Another essential color in the Hygge color scheme is gray. Gentle, subdued grays give a room refinement and depth without becoming overpowering. Because of their adaptability, gray tones can be combined with a wide range of other colors to produce a cohesive style. The use of light gray furnishings or walls can create a tranquil setting that is ideal for unwinding.

Beige, taupe, and brown are examples of earthy tones that are essential to Hygge's décor. The resemblance to natural materials such as wood, stone, and clay is strengthened by these hues. Earthy colors provide a room coziness and warmth, which helps it feel more anchored and welcoming. When paired with other neutral shades, these hues offer a unified and well-balanced aesthetic.

Gentle pastel colors like light greens, pinks, and blues can also be used to create a Hygge aesthetic. These soft hues bring a small pop of color without detracting from the tranquil atmosphere. Pastels can be utilized for items like artwork, rugs, and cushions to give a room a little flair and intrigue. To preserve the calm and comfortable ambiance that is essential to Hygge, it is crucial to choose muted, soft hues.

Hygge décor includes not only lighting, textures, and colors but also the way things are arranged and how space is used. The intention is to create a warm, inviting environment where people may unwind and rest. This frequently entails carefully placing accessories and furniture to encourage harmony and balance.

In a Hygge atmosphere, comfortable sitting is crucial. Comfortable and enticing sofas and chairs will entice guests to sit down and stay for a while. The coziness and comfort are increased by layering throws and cushions on the seats. Intimate and welcoming seating places should be a feature of furniture arrangements to encourage communication and interaction.

Incorporating personal touches is crucial to establishing a Hygge atmosphere. Sentimentally significant objects, such as heirlooms, family pictures, or trip mementos, give the décor a unique and considerable touch. These pieces add to the overall feeling of coziness and warmth, giving the area a distinctively personal touch.

Plants and flowers are typical examples of natural items utilized in Hygge décor to bring a bit of the outside in. A room with greenery feels more alive and fresh and encourages a connection to the natural world. To add color and brightness, fresh flowers can be arranged in vases or arranged on windowsills, tables, or shelves.

In conclusion, the goal of Hygge décor is to create a cozy, welcoming, and pleasant space that encourages rest and wellbeing. In order to create this atmosphere, critical components like lighting, textures, and colors are essential. An intimate ambiance is created using low-wattage bulbs, fairy lights, and candles that emit soft, pleasant lighting. Warmth and tactile appeal are added by natural, cozy materials like wood, wool, and imitation fur. A muted, neutral color scheme that draws inspiration from nature heightens the feeling of peace and quiet. A place that reflects the spirit of Hygge can be created by carefully arranging these components, offering a haven of coziness and contentment in the middle of a hectic world.

Room-by-room guide to Hygge spaces (living room, bedroom, kitchen)

More than just adhering to a set of architectural guidelines, creating Hygge spaces in your house is about creating an atmosphere that promotes coziness, happiness, and wellbeing. Hygge, a Danish word pronounced "hoo-gah," conjures up feelings of comfort, warmth, and gratitude for life's small pleasures. This section offers a thorough, room-by-room guide to establishing Hygge areas in the kitchen, living room, and bedroom. It emphasizes how these places can be altered to foster happiness and calm.

The living room serves as the focal point of the house and a space for socializing and relaxation for family and friends. The first step in designing a living space with a Hygge influence is figuring out how your furniture will be arranged. The intention is to create a cozy, welcoming environment that promotes rest and conversation. Place sofas and chairs facing each other instead of the television to encourage easy conversation. If you have the room, provide warm nooks with side tables and armchairs where people can relax and enjoy a cup of tea or an excellent book.

A crucial component of a Hygge living room is comfortable seating. Choose comfortable couches and chairs that entice you to curl up and stay a while. The secret to getting that comfortable Hygge vibe is layering. Cover the back of the couch with cozy throws and scatter a variety of neutral-colored and textured cushions. Adding warmth and coziness may be achieved very well with knitted textiles, wool, and faux fur. To further the laid-back atmosphere, think about utilizing slipcovers made of natural materials like cotton or linen.

The living room should have warm, cozy lighting rather than glaring overhead lights. Instead, to produce a soft, ambient glow, use a combination of floor lamps, table lamps, and candles. Lamps should be positioned thoughtfully to draw attention to specific sections of the space, like conversation or reading nooks. A classic component of Hygge décor, candles provide a feeling of coziness and warmth with their delicate, flickering light. Arrange them on windowsills, coffee tables, and mantelpieces to create a calm and welcoming space.

A Hygge living room's color scheme should be made up of subdued, neutral hues that promote peace and tranquility. To create a peaceful and pleasant atmosphere, soft pastels, whites, grays, and beiges are excellent color choices. The neutral background created by these hues highlights the textures and accessories. Use organic elements to give the room depth and intrigue, such as stone, wood, and wool. Whether it is painted light or dark, wooden furniture gives a feeling of coziness and stability. Think of putting in bookshelves, a coffee table, or maybe some pretty wooden trays and bowls.

In order to create a truly Hygge living area, personal touches are essential. Put sentimental objects on display, like old family photos, heirlooms, or trip mementos. These sentimental touches give the area personality and make it exclusively yours. Use indoor plants and greenery to create a natural interior atmosphere. In addition to adding a sense of vibrancy and freshness, plants help enhance wellbeing. To make a setting that is both dynamic and serene, arrange plants on windowsills, side tables, or in hanging pots.

Going on to the bedroom, the goal here should be to create a calm haven where you can relax and get a good night's sleep. As the focal point of every bedroom, let's start with the bed. Pick silky, breathable bedding made of natural materials like cotton or linen, together with a top-notch mattress. In the bedroom as in the living room, layering is crucial. Make your bed cozy and appealing by layering blankets, duvets, and sheets. Choose pastel or neutral hues that encourage peace and tranquility. A few ornamental cushions in different materials can improve the homey atmosphere.

The bedroom should have gentle, calming lighting. Use warm-toned bulbs in your bedside lamps instead of harsh overhead lighting. Think about buying lights with dimmers so you may change the brightness to suit your mood and needs. A mystical touch can also be added to the bedroom with fairy lights. To produce a lovely, glittering glow, string them along the headboard, around a mirror, or drape them over a canopy. In the bedroom, candles are also a great complement because they give a soft, flickering light that makes the space feel more peaceful.

Textures are essential when designing a bedroom that is Hygge-inspired. Select warm, inviting-to-touch materials that are soft and tactile. Layers of comfort can be added with knit throws, faux fur cushions, and woolen blankets. A cozy rug by the bed can offer a comfortable, heated surface for stepping onto in the morning. When choosing furniture and accessories, think about utilizing organic materials like wood and wicker. A wicker laundry basket, a wooden bench at the foot of the bed, or a wooden bedside table can all contribute to the homey, rustic appeal.

The bedroom's color palette ought to be soothing and tranquil. Whites, grays, and beiges are examples of neutral colors that work well because they provide a calm atmosphere that encourages sound sleep. Another option for adding a little color without overpowering the room is to use soft pastels. Maintaining a modest and straightforward palette allows the textures and materials to draw the eye and add depth and interest. Additionally, natural features like plants can heighten the feeling of peace. To add a little greenery and freshness, choose low-maintenance indoor plants that do well in low light and arrange them on windowsills, bedside tables, or shelves.

An additional crucial component of a Hygge bedroom is storage. Make an effort to maintain the area neat and orderly because clutter can be a source of stress. Keep things out of sight by storing them in bins, crates, and baskets. To optimize space and prevent clutter, choose for multipurpose furniture like a storage bench or a bed featuring built-in drawers. Books, plants, and other objects can also be displayed on open shelving to give a personal touch without taking over the room.

Another essential space for establishing Hygge in your house is the kitchen. It's a place where food is cooked and shared; therefore, it ought to make people feel cozy and connected. Start by thinking about how your kitchen is laid out and how it works. The idea is to create a room where you can enjoy cooking and spending time with loved ones while still being functional and welcoming. Make sure everything you need is easily accessible in your kitchen, which is well-arranged and free of clutter.

The kitchen's lighting should be both able to create a cozy and welcoming ambiance and bright enough to make cooking easier. To achieve a balanced look, use task lighting—such as pendant lights over work areas and under cabinet lights—in conjunction with ambient lighting. Warm-toned pendant lights may give the kitchen a pleasant glow that makes it seem cozier. Candles can also be used in the kitchen to create a comfortable, intimate atmosphere, especially during dinner parties or evening meals.

The kitchen should have textures that are both cozy and useful. Wooden surfaces, including shelves, chopping boards, and counters, give the room a comfortable, natural feel. Think of showcasing lovely equipment on open shelving, such as wooden spoons, glass jars, and ceramic bowls. These objects can be ornamental or practical, and they lend a personal touch. To enhance the overall feeling of comfort, textiles like dish towels, aprons, and tablecloths should be soft and natural. To intensify the Hygge vibe, choose for neutral or pastel-colored textiles like cotton or linen.

The kitchen should have a light and airy color scheme to create a tidy and welcoming space. For walls and cabinets, neutral hues like white, cream, and light gray are perfect since they set the stage for other pieces to stand out. To give warmth and depth, earthy tones like beige, taupe, and light greens can also be employed. To create a feeling of peace and tranquility, it's essential to keep the color scheme muted and mild. A colorful fruit bowl or a smattering of potted herbs are two colorful accessories that can add interest without overpowering the area.

In the kitchen, too, personal touches matter. Put sentimental objects on display, such as heirloom kitchenware, family recipes, or trip mementos. These accent pieces give the room personality and a very personal vibe. To add a bit of nature indoors, include natural items like potted herbs or fresh flowers. These components not only provide color and vitality but they also enhance wellbeing.

For a Hygge kitchen to remain tidy and clutter-free, storage is essential. To store goods neatly and conveniently, use baskets, jars, and other containers. Beautiful cookware can be displayed on open shelving and kept easily accessible. If you want to maximize space and maintain a clean kitchen, think about utilizing multipurpose furniture, like a kitchen island with storage.

In conclusion, designing Hygge areas in your house entails giving careful thought to the design, lighting, materials, hues, and finishing touches in each location. Use cozy seating, gentle lighting, and a muted color scheme to create a comfortable and welcoming ambiance in the living area. Create a tranquil haven in your bedroom by using breathable, soft bedding, peaceful lighting, and peaceful hues. Use natural materials, gentle lighting, and personal touches to create a warm and inviting kitchen that combines functionality and comfort. By adding these components, you may turn your house into a haven of coziness and wellbeing, emulating the spirit of Hygge and encouraging happiness and calm in daily life.

The role of personal items and memories in creating coziness

The Danish word "hygge," which describes coziness, goes beyond simple physical comfort. It is a feeling of warmth and happiness that is usually connected to easy pleasures and a sense of community. Adding sentimental objects and recollections to our living areas is one of the most meaningful methods to create this feeling of comfort. These components give our spaces a distinct personality, nostalgic feel, and character that generic décor cannot match. This section investigates the significance of sentimental objects and recollections in fostering coziness, looking at how they affect the ambiance, psychological health, and sense of self in a house.

Coziness is really about feeling safe and secure, and personal belongings are intrinsically linked to these emotions. Sentimental goods, including old family relics, pictures, and mementos from essential life moments, act as concrete memories of our individual pasts and relationships. They provide us with a sense of continuity and security by serving as anchors to our past. A quilt that has been passed down through the years, for example, is more than just a piece of cloth; it is a storehouse of love and family history that offers both emotional and physical warmth.

One of the most effective types of personal belongings that might inspire warmth is photographs. Having family photos on display in the house acts as a continual reminder of the connections that influence our lives. These photos document happy times, family time, and significant events, weaving an emotional tapestry throughout our everyday lives. A priceless snapshot can bring back memories and joy right away, easing tension and strengthening a sense of security and belonging. One of the main components of the comfortable ambiance that many people want to establish in their homes is this emotional connection.

Memorabilia from trips and significant life events is another type of personal artifacts that provide comfort. Postcards, souvenirs, and keepsakes from trips or noteworthy occasions act as tangible representations of our experiences and triumphs. These objects not only adorn our environments but also serve as living histories of the places and experiences we have been. They can remind us of the diversity and beauty of the world and evoke feelings of delight, accomplishment, and nostalgia. For example, a wall covered in maps and trip photos or a shelf filled with seashells from a beach vacation might bring back the warmth of those memories and give the area a more unique and homey vibe.

Cozy environments are also greatly enhanced by books, especially ones with sentimental value. A well-curated book library can reveal a person's passions, interests, and intellectual development. Cozy and intimate atmospheres are produced by bookshelves brimming with beloved and well-read novels. Since these books are symbols of learning, escape, and personal growth, their very existence can be consoling. A favorite book can add to a room's general comfort by bringing peace and enjoyment, whether you're reading it or just admiring it on the shelf.

Handmade goods, whether one makes them oneself or receives them from others, work very well to create a comfortable atmosphere. Mass-produced goods are unable to match the distinct energy and personal touch that these objects possess. In addition to being useful ornamental objects, hand-knit blankets, friend-made pottery, and family-created paintings are also symbols of thought, labor, and imagination. They provide warmth and character to the room, giving it a more intimate and welcoming sense. The act of producing something by hand or receiving a homemade present fortifies bonds and forges enduring memories, which adds to the home's comfort.

Apart from material objects, adding aspects that arouse memories of previous encounters can significantly enhance the coziness of the space. Scent has the ability to strongly elicit memories and feelings. A particular scent has the power to take us back in time and place, bringing with it sentiments of warmth and nostalgia. Comforting fragrances that bring back memories of joyful moments spent with loved ones can permeate the house when scented candles, essential oils, or even tried-and-true recipes are prepared. A favorite dish, a scent of freshly baked cookies, or a certain kind of flower can all combine to create a pleasant, welcoming atmosphere in a room.

Another aspect that can strengthen comfort and bring back strong memories is music. Playing music that has special meaning for us can take us back to various points in our lives and bring back memories and feelings connected to those experiences. A nostalgic and cozy ambiance can be produced with a playlist of your best songs, the soundtrack to a beloved film, or a specific song. A warm, familiar feeling that is enhanced by the sound of music can permeate the room and add to its overall friendliness.

In the home, textiles and fabrics are also essential for establishing a comfortable ambiance, particularly if they hold sentimental value. Stories and connections are carried by handcrafted blankets, quilts, and cushions that have been handed down through the centuries. Comforting oneself with a grandmother's quilt or leaning on a family member's embroidered cushion can offer emotional as well as physical relief. These fabrics take on symbolic meanings of tenderness and affection, providing a material link to dear ones and treasured recollections.

In order to create a pleasant atmosphere, personal objects should be arranged and displayed correctly. By carefully placing these things, you can make them more visible and easily accessible while also making sure they add to the general atmosphere of the room. One way to make a gallery wall stand out in a space and start a conversation is to arrange a variety of family portraits, artwork, and memories on it. The comfort of the area can be increased by placing objects on shelves, mantels, and tables in a way that tells a tale or emphasizes their significance.

Coziness can also be improved by incorporating natural components into the house, especially if those materials hold special meaning for you. A sensation of peace and oneness with nature can be evoked by flowers, plants, and organic elements like wood and stone. Layers of meaning and warmth can be added to the space with a wooden piece crafted by a family member; flowers plucked from a favorite garden, or a plant that was a present from a friend. These features not only add beauty to the house but also serve as a link to our past and the natural environment.

Making a comfortable house is a very personal and significant undertaking in and of itself. Personal organizing, rearranging, and decorating projects can be gratifying and soothing endeavors. Through this approach, people can express their creativity, think back on their own experiences, and design a space that accurately captures their personalities and ideals. Mindfulness can be practiced by carefully positioning and arranging personal belongings, which can foster a sense of present-moment awareness and gratitude for the small comforts of home.

Furthermore, having sentimental belongings and recollections in one's house might improve mental and emotional wellness. In addition to offering consolation during trying times, having sentimental items and mementos of good moments around one can inspire and motivate oneself. When things are unknown or change, these objects can serve as emotional anchors, offering comfort and stability. They provide a sense of calm and well-being by providing a sense of continuity and connection, which can help lower tension and anxiety.

In order to create comfort and a sense of community and connection, personal items and memories play a crucial role. By putting sentimental objects on display, family, and friends can feel more connected to one another and develop a shared sense of history via the sharing of personal experiences and recollections. Having events in a house with personal touches can increase guests' sense of coziness and togetherness by making them feel more at ease and welcome. The idea of hygge, which emphasizes the value of relationships and community in building a happy and comfortable life, is based on these shared experiences and connections.

Personal belongings and recollections can also add to a home's own personality and originality. Every person has a different assortment of sentimental items and items that represent their ideals, hobbies, and life experiences. A house becomes a true reflection of its occupants when it is imbued with uniqueness. Not only is a home with personal touches more intriguing and captivating, but it is also cozier and friendlier. It narrates a tale and provides details about the people that reside there, their personalities, and daily lives.

Seasonal decorating is another idea that emphasizes the importance of memories and sentimental objects in fostering warmth. The warmth of the house can be improved, and a sense of rhythm and anticipation can be created by altering the décor to suit the various seasons and festivals. One way to create a festive and comfortable atmosphere is by pulling out holiday decorations that you have accumulated over the years. This might bring back memories of prior celebrations. Seasonal accents can enhance the feeling of being outside and the passage of time. Examples of such accents include autumn leaves, winter pinecones, and spring flowers.

In summary, sentimental objects and recollections are essential to furnishing a comfortable house. They give our rooms a distinct character, nostalgic feel, and personal touch that is impossible to achieve with just generic décor. We build an environment rich in emotional connections and personal history when we surround ourselves with precious goods. These things provide us comfort and a feeling of community because they serve as concrete memories of our accomplishments, relationships, and experiences. Our houses become actual havens of coziness and warmth when we fill them with sentimental objects and memories that improve our emotional health and sense of community and connection. A home that has thoughtfully included personal touches—whether in the form of books, homemade goods, photographs, or natural elements—becomes not only aesthetically pleasing but also incredibly meaningful and welcoming.

CHAPTER III

Hygge Through the Seasons

Embracing the cold and darkness (candles, blankets, hot drinks)

Accepting the darkness and cold, especially during the protracted winter months, can have a transforming effect on how we view these difficult times of the year. We can develop methods to bring warmth, comfort, and joy during these times rather than seeing them as uncomfortable and depressing times. This section looks at several ways to welcome the cold and dark, with a particular emphasis on employing blankets, candles, and hot beverages to create a cozy and comfortable atmosphere.

When the days get shorter and the temperature drops, we tend to naturally gravitate toward light and warmth. There are many ways to satisfy this natural reaction, but using candles is one of the deepest. Since ancient times, candles have provided warmth and light, and their gentle, flickering glow can foster a peaceful, cozy ambiance. Just lighting a candle can completely change a space by creating a comfortable, welcoming glow that stands in stark contrast to the darkness and cold outside. Candles are an essential part of winter celebrations and customs in many cultures, representing warmth, light, and hope.

There is a profound psychological effect of candlelight. A candle's soft flicker and warm colors can have a relaxing impact that eases tension and encourages rest. This is especially crucial in the winter when the absence of natural light can have a negative effect on our energy and attitude. During this time, seasonal affective disorder (SAD), which is typified by depressive and lethargic symptoms, is a prevalent disease. Candles can help offset these impacts by adding more light to our living areas, which promotes comfort and wellbeing. Additionally, lighting candles can turn into a contemplative practice that helps us to slow down and appreciate the present.

Adding candles to our everyday routines can improve the feeling of warmth and friendliness in our houses. A steady, reassuring glow can be created in the home by arranging candles thoughtfully, especially in the areas where we spend the most time. Candles in the bathroom may provide a beautiful, spa-like atmosphere for a bath, while candles on the dining table can make every meal feel special. This technique takes on a new dimension when scented candles are used since they can fill the room with calming scents that promote relaxation and overall wellbeing. Aromas such as lavender, vanilla, and cedarwood are especially useful in fostering a warm and welcoming environment.

Another necessary component for enjoying the darkness and cold is blankets. Immediate physical comfort can be obtained from a soft, warm blanket that envelops us in a secure and cozy cocoon. A comfortable blanket can provide a calming tactile experience that helps ease the discomfort of cold weather. In addition, blankets have a metaphorical meaning that evokes childhood feelings of safety and nurturing—being swaddled. This psychologically significant link to early sources of comfort might foster emotions of serenity and relaxation.

When choosing blankets for optimal coziness, the selection of materials is essential. The best materials are natural fibers like cotton, wool, and cashmere because they breathe well and offer superior insulation. In particular, wool blankets are well known for their capacity to hold heat while letting moisture escape, keeping us toasty without being too hot. A blanket's texture and weight also add to its reassuring properties. The use of weighted blankets, which have grown in popularity recently, can reduce anxiety and enhance sleep quality by applying a light, even pressure that can simulate being held or embraced.

Blankets have many uses, but they may also be ornamental accents that improve the aesthetics of our living areas. A space can be made to seem more visually appealing and inviting to relax by layering various textures and colors to provide depth and intrigue. Throw blankets placed over couches, chairs, and mattresses add to the overall cozy atmosphere while also making warmth easily accessible. Incorporating seasonal themes and personal style into patterns and colors enables us to design a visually captivating and comfortable space.

Another effective aid for enjoying the winter and darkness is hot beverages. A hot beverage can be prepared and enjoyed ritualistically, which can be a very reassuring experience that brings comfort to the body and mind. Whether it's a hot chocolate, mulled wine, cider, or any other seasonal beverage, these beverages offer a sensory experience that can uplift our moods and give us a brief break from the cold.

With its wide range of tastes and types, tea is exceptionally well-liked in the winter. Herbal teas with calming qualities, such as chamomile, peppermint, and rooibos, can aid in fostering calm and rest. In addition to giving a mild caffeine boost, green and black teas provide a reassuring warmth that can help fight the lethargic feeling that frequently follows shorter days. Boiling the water and steeping the leaves for tea can turn the procedure into a mindfulness and present-focused meditation.

Another classic wintertime beverage is hot chocolate, which has a thick, velvety texture and opulent taste. This beverage evokes happy memories of childhood and holiday customs, making one feel sentimental and joyful. A profound sense of comfort and enduring memories can be made from the simple pleasure of drinking hot chocolate by the fire or after spending the day in the snow. Spices like nutmeg or cinnamon, or even a little liquor, can enhance the flavor and give this traditional drink a distinctive, customized edge.

For numerous individuals, coffee serves as a vital component of their everyday regimen, offering warmth and a much-needed energy surge. Specialty coffee beverages like lattes and mochas, which combine comfort and indulgence, become incredibly tempting in the winter. Seasonal drinks provide a festive element that can heighten the feeling of the colder months, such as peppermint mochas or pumpkin spice lattes. A warm, inviting aroma from freshly made coffee can permeate the entire house, adding to its overall comfort.

Traditionally served throughout the winter months, mulled wine and cider provide warmth and cheer. These fragrant and celebratory drinks are made with spices like star anise, cinnamon, and cloves, and occasionally with citrus added. Whether it is made in a slow cooker or on the stovetop, the aroma of freshly made mulled wine or cider can permeate the house, fostering a festive and welcoming mood. Having these drinks with loved ones can strengthen bonds between people and foster a sense of warmth and comfort on a physical and emotional level.

By incorporating these things into our daily lives—candles, blankets, and hot beverages—we may learn to appreciate the cold and darkness and change our perspective of winter from one of hardship to one of coziness and connection. By establishing routines around these exercises, we may increase their impact and provide our daily lives with more purposeful and thoughtful moments.

The Danish idea of hygge perfectly captures this way of life in the winter. Hygge places a strong emphasis on the value of establishing a cozy and welcoming environment, taking delight in small pleasures, and encouraging a sense of belonging. This kind of thinking can be especially helpful in guiding us through the difficulties of winter by giving us a structure for accepting the season with joy and grace.

Never undervalue the social benefits of embracing the dark and cold. Spending time with loved ones in a warm, candlelit space while sharing hot beverages and blankets can fortify bonds and produce enduring memories. The physical cold and darkness outside can be balanced by the mental warmth that these times of connection give.

Being aware of our physical space is another aspect of creating a warm space. Our houses can become more peaceful and orderly by decluttering and arranging them, which makes it simpler to unwind and take pleasure in the warmth and light we bring in. The general feeling of comfort can be increased by carefully placing furniture to create warm and inviting settings. Natural components like wood and plants can also bring a little bit of the outside in, resulting in a space that is harmonic and well-balanced.

In order to embrace the cold and darkness, self-care is also crucial. Whether it's with a warm bath, a good book, or a quiet time for introspection, taking the time to care for ourselves during the winter can help us stay well. Adding routines like yoga, meditation, or journaling can provide more layers of solace and stability, enabling us to face the season with grace and resiliency.

In summary, enjoying the cold and darkness requires a multimodal strategy that includes mindful practices, physical warmth, and emotional comfort. During the winter, we can improve our well-being and change our living spaces with the help of powerful instruments like candles, blankets, and hot beverages. Through the development of rituals and the integration of these aspects into our everyday existence, we can foster a feeling of comfort and happiness that surpasses the difficulties of the season. Accepting the hygge lifestyle and its tenets can direct us through this process and assist us in discovering comfort and beauty in the most basic pleasures. In the end, we can find new ways to connect with ourselves and others by embracing the cold and darkness, which will result in a deep and satisfying experience that will last us through the winter and beyond.

Festive and holiday traditions

Holiday and celebration customs are essential to human civilization because they provide a diverse range of customs, festivities, and group pursuits that unite people in contemplation and delight. These customs are found in many different cultures and religions, and each has its own distinct rituals, symbols, and interpretations. This section investigates the wide range of celebratory and holiday customs observed globally, exploring their historical roots, cultural relevance, and ongoing influence on our lives.

Christmas is one of the most extensively observed holidays in the world, with millions of people, both religious and secular, celebrating it on December 25. In Christian tradition, Christmas celebrates the birth of Jesus Christ, but in modern times, a variety of customs and practices are combined to mark the day. Ancient winter celebrations like the Roman Saturnalia, a period of feasting, gift-giving, and revelry, are where Christmas got its start. These heathen customs were able to blend with Christian doctrine when Christmas was adopted by the early Christian church, giving rise to the varied celebrations that we celebrate today.

The custom of decorating a Christmas tree is a significant part of the holiday season and is thought to have started in Germany in the sixteenth century. In the bleakest days of winter, the tree—often a fir or pine—is decked out with lights, decorations, and tinsel, signifying life and hope. The custom of exchanging gifts at Christmas is another important aspect of the holiday. It is modeled after the gifts that the Magi delivered to the infant Jesus in Christian legend. Giving gifts to family and friends helps to improve ties between them by encouraging an attitude of kindness and generosity.

Festive dinners are another way that Christmas is observed, and every culture has its own special foods. A typical Christmas meal in the US and the UK can consist of roast turkey, stuffing, and a variety of sides, followed by desserts such as mince pies and Christmas pudding. A beloved tradition in Italy, the Feast of the Seven Fishes is a variety of fish dishes served on Christmas Eve. These dinners are about more than simply the cuisine; they're also about spending time with loved ones, telling tales, and making enduring memories.

Hanukkah sometimes called the Festival of Lights, is a significant festival that holds great cultural significance and is observed by Jews worldwide. In the second century BCE, after the Maccabean Revolt against the Seleucid Empire, the Second Temple in Jerusalem was rededicated. This event is celebrated on Hanukkah. The menorah, a nine-branched candelabrum, is the most identifiable emblem of Hanukkah. During the eight-day celebration, a new candle is lit each night, along with hymns and prayers.

Hanukkah celebrations revolve around food, with many dishes cooked in oil to represent the miracle of the oil in the Temple lasting eight days. Traditional favorites include latkes (potato pancakes) and sufganiyot (doughnuts filled with jelly). In addition, games like spinning the dreidel—a four-sided top adorned with Hebrew letters—and gift-giving, especially between kids, are part of the celebration.

Dr. Maulana Karenga established the relatively recent holiday Kwanzaa in 1966 to commemorate African history and to encourage togetherness and self-determination. It is observed from December 26 to January 1. The Nguzo Saba, or Seven Principles, are the foundation of Kwanzaa and comprise, among other things, Umoja (unity), Kujichagulia (self-determination), and Nia (purpose). Every night, one of the seven principles is represented by a candle lit on the kinara, a seven-branched candleholder.

On December 31, Kwanzaa celebrations usually include a communal feast known as Karamu, as well as music, dance, and storytelling. African Americans use the occasion as an opportunity to celebrate their cultural heritage, take stock of their group accomplishments, and look forward to the future with pride and purpose.

Millions of Hindus celebrate Diwali, often known as the Festival of Lights, which is one of the most significant Hindu holidays. Diwali represents the victory of good over evil and light over darkness. The celebration is linked to a number of gods and myths, chief among them being the epic Ramayana, which tells of Lord Rama's return to his kingdom following his victory over the evil king Ravana.

Five days are dedicated to celebrating Diwali, each with its own customs and significance. Houses are meticulously cleaned, rangoli—elegant designs created with colorful powders—decorated, and diyas—oil lamps—are lit. Cracker popping and fireworks are frequent sights, signifying the festival's excitement and vigor. Families get together for joyous feasts, which frequently feature treats like barfis and laddoos, and to exchange blessings and gifts.

Two important Islamic festivals that Muslims around the world commemorate are Eid al-Fitr and Eid al-Adha. The month of Ramadan, which is dedicated to fasting, prayer, and introspection, comes to a conclusion on Eid al-Fitr, the Festival of Breaking the Fast. A joyful dinner shared with family and friends follows the celebration, which starts with a special prayer at the mosque. In addition, Muslims use the occasion to give to the poor by participating in the Zakat al-Fitr tradition.

The Festival of Sacrifice, Eid al-Adha, honors Abraham's (Ibrahim's) willingness to offer his son as a sacrifice to God. One of the Five Pillars of Islam, the Hajj trip to Mecca, falls on the same day as the holiday. Muslims all around the world engage in the custom of offering an animal—usually a sheep or goat—for sacrifice. The meat is then shared among loved ones, close friends, and the underprivileged. The principles of community, religion, and obedience are highlighted by the festival.

Chinese New Year, or Lunar New Year, is a significant celebration that ushers in the lunar calendar and is observed in China and other Asian nations. The Lantern celebration marks the end of the festival, which usually lasts for 15 days. Many individuals travel great distances to be with their loved ones during the Lunar New Year, which is a time for family reunions. Dragon and lion dances, the distribution of red envelopes (hongbao) containing yen, and the setting off of fireworks are all part of the festivities.

Every traditional meal has a symbolic value, making it an integral element of Lunar New Year celebrations. For example, dumplings, which resemble old Chinese money in shape, stand for riches, while fish indicate abundance. Red, a hue linked to happiness and luck, is frequently used in apparel and décor.

Día de los Muertos, often known as the Day of the Dead, is a colorful and lively holiday honoring loved ones who have passed away in Mexico and other Latin American countries. The event, which is observed on November 1st and 2nd, reflects the syncretic aspect of Latin American culture by fusing Catholicism with indigenous traditions. In homes and cemeteries, altars, also known as ofrendas, are arranged and decorated with pictures, marigold flowers, candles, and the deceased's favorite meals. Traditional offerings include sugar skulls and pan de muerto, or bread of the dead.

Families get together to commemorate and honor the lives of the deceased on Día de los Muertos, which is a joyous affair rather than a melancholy one. It is thought that during these days, the spirits of the deceased come back to dwell among us, relishing in the presence of their cherished ones and the sacrifices they receive. The festivities are frequently accompanied by music, dance, and parades that emphasize the beauty and cyclical nature of life and death.

The New Year, or Shogatsu, is one of the most significant and extensively observed holidays in Japan. The celebrations usually start on January 1st and go on for a few days. Cleaning the entire house, adorning with bamboo, pine branches, and plum blossoms, and cooking special delicacies called osechi-ryori are all part of the New Year's preparations. Families appreciate these foods, which have individual symbolic meanings, artistically placed in lacquered boxes over the holiday season.

A critical custom in Japan is the ringing of temple bells on New Year's Eve at midnight, or Joya no Kane. The 108 bell rings represent the 108 earthly wants that people are said to have Buddhists, and the purpose of the ceremony is to purify the soul and start the new year with a clear head. Another significant tradition is the Hatsumode shrine visit when people offer prayers for health and prosperity for the upcoming year.

Thanksgiving is a beloved holiday observed on the fourth Thursday of November in the United States. It began as a joint harvest celebration between the Native Americans and the Pilgrims in the early 17th century, signifying appreciation for a plentiful crop and intercommunal cooperation. Thanksgiving is a time when families get together to celebrate and give thanks for all that they have in their lives. A roast turkey usually serves as the main course of Thanksgiving dinner, with sides including mashed potatoes, pumpkin pie, cranberry sauce, and stuffing.

An iconic aspect of the celebration is the Macy's Thanksgiving Day Parade in New York City, which includes enormous balloons, floats, and marching bands. Millions of Americans watch the yearly football games on Thanksgiving as another ritual. These gatherings, in addition to the shared meal, foster a sense of community and tradition that cuts beyond personal differences.

Holiday and celebratory customs involve not just joy and celebration but also introspection and thankfulness. They offer chances to stop and reflect on the value of things like family, community, and the passing of time. These customs frequently have profound symbolic connotations that uphold the moral principles and worldviews that are essential to our identities and societies.

Festive and holiday customs are deeply entwined with the natural environment and seasonal cycles in many indigenous societies. For instance, the solar God Inti is honored during the Incan festival of Inti Raymi, which is observed in Peru and corresponds to the Southern Hemisphere's winter solstice. The intricate rituals, dances, and sun offerings that are a part of the celebration highlight the close relationship that the Inca society had with the natural world.

Comparably, a Native American powwow is a joyous occasion that frequently honors significant occasions or seasons and features singing, dancing, and drumming. Native American powwows are an essential component of their culture because they give communities a place to gather, celebrate, and pass on customs to future generations.

It is impossible to exaggerate the significance of festive and holiday customs in preserving cultural continuity. These festivities frequently act as a link between generations, facilitating the sharing of artistic practices, beliefs, and information. They help people connect with their heritage and community by fostering a sense of identification and belonging.

Festive and holiday customs not only have cultural and social value, but they also have economic effects. Numerous holidays, like Christmas, New Year's, and Diwali, encourage large expenditures on travel, food, decorations, gifts, and other expenses, which helps both the local and worldwide economies. Retail, hospitality, and entertainment are just a few of the linked industries that have overgrown as a result of the commercialization of holidays.

However, there are also worries about the traditional meanings and values being lost as a result of the commercialization of holidays. Stress and financial strain might result from the urge to spend and consume, overshadowing the primary goals of these celebrations. Many civilizations struggle to strike a balance between economic interests and the preservation of cultural and spiritual importance.

Despite these obstacles, joyous and seasonal customs persist in developing and adjusting, mirroring shifting societal, financial, and cultural environments. Growing interest has been seen in recent years in both developing new customs that fit with modern values and lifestyles and revitalizing and maintaining traditional ones. For instance, an increasing awareness of environmental issues and a desire to celebrate in a way that is in harmony with nature can be seen in the emergence of sustainable and eco-friendly holiday customs.

Holiday and celebratory customs can offer chances for cross-cultural communication and understanding. People from different backgrounds frequently join together to celebrate and discover each other's holidays and customs in our more linked globe. This cross-cultural interaction can promote a deeper understanding and respect for various lifestyles, which will make society more inclusive and peaceful.

To sum up, celebrations and holiday customs are essential component of human culture that bring happiness, purpose, and community into our lives. They provide chances to honor our history, consider our principles, and deepen our ties to our families and communities. Though these customs differ significantly between countries and religions, they all center around the ideas of thankfulness, giving, and unity. In addition to honoring our history, we also foster a sense of continuity and hope for the future by embracing and upholding these traditions.

Indoor activities to enjoy during the winter months

The winter months, with their chilly temperatures, snow-covered scenery, and fewer days, have a certain allure. But the season can also present difficulties, particularly when inclement weather limits outside activities. This is a great time to discover and take part in a range of indoor activities that not only pass the time but also inspire happiness, creativity, and relaxation. We will examine a variety of indoor winter hobbies in this section, talking about their advantages and how they might improve our lives at this time of year.

One of the most stimulating things you can do inside in the cold is read. The cooler temperatures are the ideal justification for curling up with a book and losing yourself in its pages. Reading may open your eyes to new ideas, take you to new places, and broaden your horizons, regardless of whether you like to read poetry, non-fiction, or fiction. If you have lengthy books that you might not have time for during the busier months, winter is a fantastic time to read them. A comfortable chair, warm blankets, and sufficient lighting may create a nice reading nook that will make reading even more enjoyable.

Baking and cooking indoors is another fantastic wintertime hobby. What better way to satisfy our demands for comfort food throughout the winter than to cook delectable dinners and sweets at home? You can experiment with new recipes and ingredients when cooking, which can be both a creative outlet and a valuable skill. For example, baking is a favorite winter activity since it can make your home seem snug with the warmth of the oven and the perfume of freshly made food. Cooking and baking can be pretty fulfilling, whether you're creating a big pot of stew, baking some cookies, or trying your hand at making fresh bread.

Another excellent method to keep busy in the winter is with crafts and do-it-yourself projects. Taking part in artistic pursuits like woodworking, painting, knitting, or crocheting can make you feel accomplished and calm. With these crafts, you may develop new skills, show your creativity, and make handmade goods that look great as gifts or accent pieces for your house. Winter crafts are especially great for knitting and crocheting since they can be completed while cozy inside, and the finished items, such as blankets, caps, and scarves, are great for keeping warm.

Classic indoor pastimes like board games and puzzles can be enjoyed by yourself or with loved ones. They offer a great way to kill time, keep the mind active, and promote social connection. Whether you like strategy games, trivia games, or cooperative games, there is something for everyone when it comes to board games because they are available in a broad range of topics and levels of difficulty. Contrarily, puzzles present a distinct form of difficulty that calls for perseverance, focus, and problem-solving abilities. When the last piece is placed, finishing a giant jigsaw puzzle may be a gratifying and peaceful experience that gives one a sense of accomplishment.

Indoor exercise can be a terrific method to stay active during the winter months for people who enjoy being physically active. Home exercises, YOGA, and dancing are all great ways to keep in shape without going outside in the winter. You may follow along with a variety of fitness sessions from the comfort of your living room with the help of numerous online platforms. Mainly yoga helps the body and mind by encouraging strength, flexibility, and relaxation. Another enjoyable approach to get moving is by dancing, which can be done both solo and with others. Dancing is an upbeat and happy way to get in shape.

A favorite wintertime indoor pastime that provides enjoyment and relaxation is movie and TV marathons.

Whether you're more interested in documentaries, TV shows, or vintage film, there's no lack of stuff to pick from, thanks to the wide range of streaming services accessible. Making a comfortable movie-watching space with pillows, blankets, and food can improve the experience and make it a fun way to pass a chilly winter's day. This is also an excellent opportunity to revisit old favorites or catch up on series you've been meaning to watch.

Winter is a great time for music lovers to learn how to play an instrument, discover new genres, or just kick back and listen to their favorite songs. Playing an instrument can be a fulfilling and healing hobby that gives you a creative release and a sense of achievement as you advance in your abilities. Winter is an excellent time to pick up an instrument if you don't already have one, either through private instruction or online tutorials. Whether you listen to music actively or just as background noise, it can improve your mood and make your house feel cozy and welcoming.

Another fulfilling hobby that can bring a little bit of nature inside your house in the winter is indoor gardening. You can still reap the benefits of indoor plant care even though the cold may have put an end to your outdoor gardening plans. Houseplants may beautify your home, lower stress levels, and enhance the quality of the air. Winter is also a great time to start studying plants, starting indoor seed preparations, and making plans for your spring garden. Taking care of a few potted plants or creating a tiny indoor herb or vegetable garden are examples of indoor gardening.

Painting, drawing, and sculpting are examples of art and craft projects that can occupy your mind for hours on end. Engaging in these artistic pursuits not only lets you express yourself creatively but also has therapeutic effects that aid in stress reduction and mental health enhancement. Having an area set aside for art in your house with all the tools you need can make it simpler to get creative whenever inspiration strikes. Winter is a terrific season to experiment with different materials and learn new skills, whether you're a novice or an established artist.

Another indoor wintertime hobby that may be rather enjoyable is writing. Writing gives you a chance to express yourself, set objectives, and reflect on your ideas and experiences, whether you choose blogging, creative writing, or journaling. Keeping a journal can be especially helpful for mental health as it provides a means of gaining perspective and processing feelings. Poetry, short stories, and novels are examples of creative writing that let you use your imagination and hone your narrative abilities. Winter might be a great time to concentrate on writing projects because of its serene and reflective mood.

Taking up a new pastime or skill can also be a fulfilling way to pass the winter indoors. You may pursue interests in anything from foreign languages and computing to cuisine and photography thanks to the wealth of online tutorials and courses accessible. Acquiring new knowledge can give you a feeling of accomplishment and purpose, which can keep your mind busy and focused. Taking up a new pastime might also introduce you to new social circles and communities, even if they are virtual ones.

In addition to helping you unwind and revitalize, indoor hobbies can also involve pampering and self-care techniques. A spa-like environment at home with candles, aromatherapy oils, and calming music can enhance the pleasure of self-care rituals like having a bath, getting a facial, or meditating. Self-care practices can improve both physical and mental well-being and help fight the wintertime blues. You can make sure that you stay balanced and rejuvenated during the winter by making time for self-care on a regular basis.

It can also be advantageous to include mindfulness and relaxation exercises in your winter routine. Deep breathing techniques, gradual muscle relaxation, and meditation are a few practices that can help lower stress and enhance general wellbeing. The slower tempo and calmer environment of winter make it the perfect time for these exercises, which help you achieve inner serenity and a closer relationship with yourself.

Doing home renovation projects is another fun indoor thing to perform in the winter. This can include smaller jobs like clearing out drawers and closets or more significant undertakings like painting or redesigning an area. Engaging in these activities not only enhances your living space but also gives you a productive and accomplished feeling. Winter is a terrific time to finish those renovations you've been putting off because you can concentrate on making your house more livable and valuable.

Participating in social interactions, however, virtually, can aid in overcoming feelings of loneliness that arise throughout the winter season. Opportunities for social contact and connection can be found in online clubs and groups, virtual game evenings, and video conversations with friends and family. In times when in-person gatherings may be scarce, these activities play a crucial role in fostering relationships and a feeling of community.

Engaging in online lectures, webinars, or book clubs can be an excellent method for individuals who seek intellectual stimulation to stay motivated and study over the winter season. Numerous organizations and educational institutions host free or inexpensive online events on a variety of subjects. Participating in an online book club can foster intellectual and social engagement as you debate books and exchange perspectives with other members.

Wintertime indoor activities also give an opportunity to concentrate on personal development. In order to make the most of the season and prepare for a prosperous year ahead, you can create goals, make vision boards, and form new routines. Winter's reflective atmosphere promotes planning and introspection, which helps you pinpoint areas in your life that need work and move closer to your objectives.

During the winter, parents may keep their children entertained and active by choosing enjoyable indoor activities. Indoor games, science experiments, and craft projects can offer hours of entertainment and education. Family ties can be strengthened, and treasured memories can be made through baking, reading aloud, and creating forts. Winter is a great time to take things slow, spend time with your kids, discover new interests, and encourage their creativity.

During the winter, playing video games indoors may also be entertaining and pleasant. With so many games to choose from that cater to a range of interests and ability levels, gaming can be both an online social media platform and a source of amusement. While single-player games offer immersive experiences that can be demanding and soothing, cooperative and multiplayer games facilitate social engagement.

Winter is a great season for anyone who appreciates the performing arts to explore dance, theater, and music. Opportunities to study and enjoy these art forms from home are provided by virtual performances and online courses. Indulging in physical activity and artistic outlets such as singing, dancing, or playing an instrument can improve your mental and physical health. During the winter, you can also indulge your wanderlust by researching virtual trip experiences. You may visit new destinations from the comfort of your home with the help of virtual tours and experiences offered by a lot of museums, national parks, and cultural sites. These virtual encounters can stimulate future trip plans and provide educational possibilities.

To sum up, the winter season presents a unique chance to investigate a variety of indoor pursuits that can improve our quality of life and promote pleasure, relaxation, and personal development. There are lots of activities to keep yourself busy and entertained indoors, ranging from reading and cooking to creating and picking up new skills. We can make the most of the winter months by engaging in these activities, which will promote wellbeing, creativity, and connections. Wintertime indoor activities can provide us happiness and contentment, whether it is through socializing with others or engaging in solitary tasks.

CHAPTER IV

Hygge in Everyday Activities

The art of slow cooking and baking

The skill of slow cooking and baking is an expression of a culinary heritage that values attention to detail, patience, and a strong bond with the food preparation process. This ancient technique, which has been handed down through the years, provides a contrast to the convenience-driven, quick-fix cooking that characterizes much modern-day cuisine. Techniques like slow cooking and baking let flavors mingle and develop over long periods of time, producing rich, complex, and incredibly delicious foods. This section examines the many facets of slow baking and cooking, emphasizing the methodology, cultural relevance, advantages, and rising use of these approaches in modern food.

The low and slow approach is the foundation of slow cooking. This method cooks food slowly and evenly by using low temperatures over extended periods of time. The practice of slow cooking dates back to the prehistoric era, when people first learned to use fire for cooking. Early techniques included heating food in a clay vessel that contained heat and steam to simmer it and pit roasting, which involved burying food under hot coals. Not only were these methods appropriate at the time, but they also produced dishes that were delicate and tasty.

These days, slow cooking is almost always associated with Dutch ovens and slow cookers. Crock-pots, another name for slow cookers, became well-liked in the middle of the 20th century as a practical meal-preparation tool for working families. These electric cookers are perfect for braising meats and stews since they keep the temperature consistently low. The Dutch oven is a multipurpose, heavy cast-iron pot that works well in the oven as well as on the cooktop. It is ideal for slow-cooking a range of foods, including roasts and casseroles, due to its capacity to hold and transfer heat evenly.

The rich flavor of food simmered is one of its distinguishing features. The longer cooking time facilitates the breakdown of proteins and complex carbs, giving the food a savory, deep flavor. This technique also makes it easier for the flavors of various ingredients to combine, resulting in a dish that is balanced and harmonious. For example, soft beef stew slowly absorbs the tastes of the vegetables, herbs, and spices, resulting in a merging of flavors that are challenging to produce using rapid cooking techniques.

Apart from taste, slow cooking has valuable advantages. It's a quick and effective method for giving difficult meat slices a juicy, delicious texture. Additionally, an extensive range of ingredients, including ones that might usually go to waste, can be used with this technique. Slow cooking can be a cost-effective and environmentally friendly method of meal preparation by using seasonal vegetables and cheap cuts of meat. Additionally, because slow cooking is a hands-off method, the cook can allow the food to simmer after the initial preparation is complete, freeing up time for other pursuits.

Similar to slow cooking, baking has a long and illustrious history that goes back thousands of years. The first baked goods were basic flatbreads that were heated on stones. Oven technology advanced over time, enabling the creation of increasingly complex baked items, including cakes, pastries, and leavened bread. Baking evokes memories of family kitchens filled with the comforting aroma of freshly baked bread or cookies and is frequently connected with tradition and coziness.

Both patience and accuracy are necessary during baking. Baking depends on precise measures and temperature, unlike other cooking techniques where changes can be made as needed. These specific conditions are required for the chemical reactions that take place during baking, such as the browning of the crust or the activity of yeast. Because of this, baking is both an art and a science, relying as much on intuition and experience as on technical know-how.

The sourdough method is one of the distinguishing features of slow baking. The natural fermentation process used to make sourdough bread depends on bacteria and wild yeast. From cultivating and preserving a starter culture to the last bake, this procedure can take many days. The end product is a chewy, open-crumb bread with a nuanced flavor. In recent years, there has been a rebirth of sourdough baking, with many homebakers developing their own starters and honing their techniques.

The use of long fermentation times for doughs is another facet of slow baking. With this technique, which is frequently employed in the baking of artisan bread, more decadent flavors and superior texture can be developed. Complex carbohydrates are also broken down by the prolonged fermentation process, which facilitates more straightforward digestion of the bread. By enhancing gluten development and hydration, methods like autolyze —in which flour and water are combined and left to rest before adding yeast and salt—further improve the finished product.

It is impossible to exaggerate the cultural significance of baking and slow cooking. Many nations all around the world have strong culinary traditions that are ingrained in these techniques. Slow cooking is exemplified by the classic French meals coq au vin and boeuf bourguignon, for instance. To get the distinctive depth of flavor in these recipes, they must simmer for hours. Bolognese sauce, or slow-cooked ragù, is a mainstay of Italian food that exemplifies the advantages of long cooking times.

Traditional baking methods have been conserved and transmitted down the centuries. The craft of baking is highly valued in nations like Germany and Austria, where specific delayed fermentation procedures are needed to create delicacies like rye bread and pretzels. Similarly, slow fermentation and careful baking are critical components of the Japanese method for creating shokupan, a soft and fluffy white bread with a distinct flavor and texture.

Slow baking and cooking have advantages beyond flavor and texture. These techniques promote preparing food with greater awareness and purpose. Taking the time to leisurely cook or bake may be a kind of self-care and a method to establish a connection with the food we eat in a world where convenience frequently wins out over quality. It enables chefs to interact with the ingredients, comprehend their qualities, and recognize the changes that take place while they cook.

Additionally, baking and slow cooking can promote a sense of solidarity and community. Memories and deep relationships can be made when family and friends gather for a freshly baked loaf of bread or a slow-cooked meal. Cooking with care and slowness may also be a contemplative technique that makes you feel accomplished and satisfied.

A resurgence of interest in slow baking and cooking has occurred recently, partly due to increased consciousness of the significance of ethical and sustainable food practices. Using whole ingredients, minimizing processed foods, and supporting local producers are all in line with the principles of slow cooking and baking, which offer a way to reduce waste and maximize available resources as people become more aware of the environmental impact of their food choices.

These techniques have also been greatly assisted by the slow food movement, which had its start in Italy in the latter half of the 20th century. The movement promotes a return to more conventional methods of food preparation, placing an emphasis on sustainability, quality, and the preservation of cultural traditions. This ideology places a strong focus on slow cooking and baking since they uphold the principles of taking your time, respecting the ingredients, and having fun while cooking.

The popularity of slow cooking and baking has increased due to the growth of digital media and the internet. Social media and online platforms have facilitated the sharing of experiences, skills, and recipes among aficionados. Slow baking and cooking blogs, YouTube channels, and Instagram profiles have garnered a sizable fan base, forming online communities of like-minded people. The ease of accessibility of these methods has helped to demystify them and encouraged a new generation of home cooks to join the slow food movement.

Although slow cooking and baking have numerous advantages and delights, these techniques are not without difficulties. Those with hectic schedules may find it challenging to make the necessary time commitment. Furthermore, there may be a high learning curve because these procedures frequently call for a degree of expertise and experience that is intimidating for novices. Nonetheless, the benefits are definitely worth the effort with patience and practice.

In summary, the skill of slow cooking and baking is evidence of the importance of attention, patience, and a strong bond with the cooking process. These time-honored techniques provide a complex and sophisticated approach to food preparation that is sometimes overlooked in the hectic modern world. They are based on custom and cultural legacy. We may attain unmatched flavors and textures, develop a deeper appreciation for the food we eat, and forge deep bonds with the people we spend our meals with by taking our time when cooking and baking. The fact that people are becoming more interested in slow baking and cooking is a good indication that more people are realizing the value of these methods for community, sustainability, and mindfulness, in addition to their culinary advantages. We respect the customs of the past while fostering the creation of fresh, enduring memories for the future as we investigate and appreciate the art of slow cooking and baking.

Creating rituals around meals and beverages

It is a behavior that is deeply ingrained in the human experience and crosses cultural and temporal boundaries to create rituals around meals and drinks. These customs have a variety of functions, such as establishing a sense of belonging and community as well as giving daily life shape and purpose. At their core, they represent the significance of food and drink in our lives, whether they are complex or essential, private or public. This section examines the customs around meals and drinks, including their historical origins, cultural relevance, psychological advantages, and contemporary modifications.

Food and drink rituals have always played a significant role in religious and cultural customs, according to H. Meals served multiple purposes in ancient societies, including celebrations of essential occasions and deity adoration in addition to providing nourishment. For instance, during the communal feasts known as symposia in ancient Greece, attendees participated in rites that included making offerings to the gods and philosophical conversations. Similar to this, extravagant feasts were a symbol of social standing and riches in ancient Rome, frequently complete with ornate rituals and ceremonies.

Worldwide religious traditions have also created distinct customs related to food and drink. As a sacred ritual representing the body and blood of Christ, the sharing of bread and wine during the Eucharist promotes a sense of spiritual solidarity among Christians. The Passover Seder is a ceremonial supper celebrated in Judaism to remember the Exodus from Egypt. It involves particular dishes and customs that have both religious and historical importance. Islamic cultures celebrate Ramadan, a month-long fast from sunrise to sunset, which culminates in the iftar meal, an evening gathering with rituals and a chance to break the fast.

Beyond religious contexts, food and beverage rituals have cultural significance. These customs are essential to social cohesiveness and cultural identity in many countries. One highly ritualized practice that promotes harmony, respect, purity, and peace is the Japanese tea ceremony or chanoyu. It is a kind of meditation and aesthetic appreciation that entails the careful preparation and presentation of matcha, or powdered green tea. The goal of the tea ceremony is to help participants develop a strong sense of connection and mindfulness in addition to enjoying tea.

Offering food to gods, or prasadam, is a significant tradition that represents gratitude and devotion in India. After the food is provided, it is divided among the followers, fostering a shared experience that strengthens ties between the group. Comparably, communal meals play a significant role in social life in many African cultures, where customs around them promote hospitality, sharing, and the development of relationships between the family and community.

There is ample evidence supporting the psychological advantages of establishing rituals around meals and drinks. These customs offer a feeling of order and regularity, which is incredibly reassuring during stressful or uncertain situations. Ritualistic actions can also improve the sensory experience of eating and drinking, adding to the pleasure and satisfaction of these activities. Rituals have been found to improve awareness and enable people to relish their food and drink and be more mindful of the current moment.

Additionally, meal and drink routines can be pretty crucial for mental and physical health. They can offer consistency and steadiness, particularly during turbulent or changing times. Family customs, like holiday feasts or Sunday dinners, might, for instance, produce enduring memories and a sense of community. Since cooking and sharing food is a manner of caring for and supporting others, these rituals can also be used as a way to show love and care.

Modern society's fast-paced lifestyle frequently causes meal and drink rituals to be less critical. The popularity of dining alone, fast food culture, and hectic schedules have all led to a fall in customs. But there is a growing push to revive and update traditional rites for contemporary living. This renaissance stems from an understanding of the advantages of mindful eating, leisurely cuisine, and the value of community and connection.

The farm-to-table movement, which prioritizes ingredients that are acquired locally, sustainably, and ethically, is one instance of a modern adaption. This strategy fosters a closer relationship between ourselves and the food we eat while also helping local farmers and lessening the impact on the environment. Farm-to-table restaurants encourage mindfulness and appreciation of the ingredients through rituals that highlight their origins and journey during the dining experience.

The popularity of wine and cheese or beer and food pairings, for example, has led to a resurgence of interest in the ceremonial elements of dining. These gatherings are frequently designed to bring out the best in food and wine, resulting in a multisensory ritual that elevates the act of eating and drinking. Pairing events and guided tastings have the potential to develop into social rituals that unite individuals in the exploration and appreciation of culinary arts.

Within the beverage industry, new customs have been established as a result of the growing appeal of specialty coffee and artisan cocktails. Craft cocktail establishments frequently highlight the skill and attention to detail that go into creating drinks, with bartenders going through lengthy rituals to make and serve each drink. Because of this, drinking becomes a theatrical and intensely exciting experience. Similar to this, specialty coffee shops frequently highlight brewing rituals; techniques like pour-over and siphon brewing are integrated into the customer experience, promoting a greater understanding of the art of coffee manufacturing.

Families and individuals are increasingly finding ways to create rituals around their meals and drinks at home. Some people might do this by scheduling a weekly family dinner in which everyone helps prepare and eats together.

Some people establish personal rituals, like making the ideal cup of coffee in the morning and sipping it slowly before beginning the day. These tiny, deliberate actions have the power to turn routine events into heartfelt rituals that offer consolation, happiness, and a sense of community.

The way we establish and communicate food and drink traditions has also been impacted by the digital era. There are a ton of photos and inspirations for exquisitely arranged tables, inventive cuisine, and distinctive eating experiences on social media sites like Instagram and Pinterest. In situations when in-person meetings are not feasible, virtual get-togethers—like online cooking classes or virtual wine tastings—have gained popularity as a means of fostering relationships and sharing culinary customs.

Another contemporary take on meal rituals is the idea of mindful eating, which encourages people to focus entirely on the eating and drinking experience. Slowing down, enjoying the sensory components of food, and being conscious of your body's signals of hunger and fullness are standard components of mindful eating practices. This method encourages better eating habits and a more positive relationship with food in addition to making meals more enjoyable.

Future-focused rituals centered around food and drink will undoubtedly continue to change and adapt to shifting cultural settings and lifestyles. But the fundamental ideas behind these practices—community, awareness, appreciation, and connection—never go out of style. Meal and beverage routines, whether established through time-honored customs or updated for contemporary tastes, have the power to profoundly improve our lives.

In summary, developing customs surrounding meals and drinks is a deeply ingrained habit in human history and society. These customs improve the sensory and emotional aspects of eating and drinking while also fostering connection, order, and significance. The significance of these rites is still apparent, whether they are part of contemporary customs or old religious ceremonies. The deliberate development and modification of meal and beverage rituals can provide a means to intentionally slow down, establish connections with people, and discover joy and significance in the essential act of sharing food and drink as we manage the complexity of modern life. These rituals, which might involve innovative culinary experiences, mindful eating techniques, or traditional family meals, have the capacity to profoundly alter our connection with food and with one another while fostering enduring memories and a sense of community.

Enjoying simple pleasures in food and drink

The idea of "enjoying simple pleasures in food and drink" encourages us to appreciate these basic pleasures of eating and drinking without being distracted by the hectic pace of modern life. This way of thinking promotes mindfulness, an appreciation of staple foods, and a close relationship with the sensory pleasures that our food offers. This section examines the cultural significance, psychological advantages, historical underpinnings, and contemporary practices related to indulging in small pleasures like food and drink, emphasizing how doing so might improve our overall well-being.

Historically, basic pleasures in food and drink have been necessary to many cultures. Mealtime gatherings were frequently infused with a spirit of joy and togetherness in ancient societies. For example, the term "symposium" in ancient Greek meant more than just a party; it also referred to a get-together where people came to eat, drink, converse, and engage in intellectual debates while honoring the essential joy of human connection.

Comparably, communal feasts celebrating the abundance of the land and highlighting the simple pleasure of fresh, in-season products marked the harvest season in many rural civilizations.

Enjoying modest pleasures in food and drink has cultural importance that is seen all throughout the world. The idea of "la dolce vita" in Italy refers to the practice of savoring life's small pleasures, especially those associated with food and wine. This philosophy is reflected in Italian cooking, which is renowned for its simplicity and emphasis on top-notch, fresh ingredients. An example of how a few carefully chosen components can produce a dish that is both tasty and gratifying is a plate of pasta al pomodoro, which is made with just tomatoes, garlic, olive oil, and basil.

"Washoku" is a Japanese cooking technique that highlights balance and harmony while showcasing the inherent flavors of ingredients. Rice, miso soup, pickled veggies, and grilled fish are typical dishes from traditional Japanese cuisine. This minimalistic style brings out the inherent flavors of each ingredient. The "chanoyu," or Japanese tea ceremony, is another example of this regard for simplicity. Matcha, or powdered green tea, is the focal point of this highly ritualized practice, which encourages a thoughtful enjoyment of the beverage's nuanced flavors and peaceful ceremony ambiance.

Enjoying small pleasures in food and drink has significant psychological advantages. Savoring small joys is strongly related to mindfulness, a discipline that entails giving the current moment your whole attention. By approaching food and drink mindfully, we can improve our whole experience by becoming more conscious of the flavors, textures, and fragrances. Increased contentment and a better appreciation for the nourishment we get from our meals can result from this increased awareness.

Studies have demonstrated that mindful eating can encourage more healthful eating practices. People are more likely to identify feelings of hunger and fullness when they eat slowly and enjoy every meal, which can help them avoid overindulging. Additionally, by lowering tension and anxiety related to food, this method can promote a healthier relationship with eating. Rather than using food as a coping mechanism for emotions or following rigorous diets, mindful eating encourages us to pay attention to our bodies and appreciate food for its natural pleasure.

Enjoying small pleasures in food and drink can also contribute to a feeling of security and contentment. The ritual of cooking and dining can provide a sense of stability in a world that is frequently chaotic and uncertain. Cooking and eating turn into routines that give our days structure and foster peaceful, introspective periods. Feeling the warmth of a newly made loaf of bread, eating ripe fruit, or enjoying a cup of herbal tea can all be sensory experiences that promote contentment and serenity.

The fast-paced nature of modern living has led to an evolution in the ways that people enjoy the small pleasures of food and drink. The late 20th-century Italian-founded slow food movement promotes a return to traditional cooking techniques, regional foods, and unhurried meals. By promoting a more leisurely approach to food preparation and consumption, this movement helps people develop stronger bonds with the people they eat with and the sources of their food.

Another contemporary trend that highlights the value of using fresh, locally sourced ingredients is farm-to-table dining. This strategy not only improves the taste and nutritional content of meals but also helps regional farmers and lessens the environmental effect of food production. Farm-to-table eateries frequently emphasize straightforward cooking methods that highlight the inherent flavors of the products and reaffirm the delight of experiencing food in its most unadulterated state.

A growing number of people are rediscovering the joy of cooking at home. People now have easier access to fresh, in-season vegetables because of the growth of community-supported agriculture (CSA) programs and home gardening. Cooking using locally grown or obtained products can be incredibly fulfilling and can help one develop a stronger appreciation for the work that goes into creating food, as well as a sense of connection to the land.

A growing trend in cooking and dining is the minimalist lifestyle. In the kitchen, minimalism entails staying away from processed foods and excessively complicated recipes in favor of key ingredients and methods. This method, which stresses the quality and inherent flavors of ingredients, is in line with the philosophy of savoring life's small pleasures. Cooking minimalistically inspires people to be inventive and resourceful, maximizing what they already have and appreciating the beauty of simplicity.

Within the beverage industry, there is an increasing recognition of the creativity and skill required to produce superior drinks. For instance, the emergence of specialty coffee culture has increased attention to the subtleties of coffee beans, brewing techniques, and the whole sensory experience of consuming coffee. Similar to this, the craft beer movement offers a wide variety of flavors and types that may be savored and enjoyed, celebrating the ingenuity and expertise of brewers.

There is a resurgence of tea culture, which has a long history in various regions of the world. People are regaining interest in the vast world of tea as they explore anything from modern tea tastings to traditional Chinese tea ceremonies. Making and enjoying tea is a peaceful and calming activity that gives one a chance to slow down and savor the small pleasures of a perfectly made cup.

There has been a change in wine culture as well, with a focus on terroir and handcrafted wines. People can taste the unique qualities of various varietals and learn about the winemaking process through wine tastings and vineyard excursions. By emphasizing the sensory experience of wine, this approach elevates the pleasure of every mouthful and transforms drinking into a ritual that honors the relationship between the vineyard, the winemaker, and the customer.

Another technique to improve the enjoyment of small pleasures is to establish rituals around meals and drinks. Rituals provide daily actions shape and significance, transforming them into memorable occasions. For instance, putting candles on the table, arranging it attractively, and turning on some relaxing music may turn a simple dinner into something special. Eating and drinking can be elevated to a more intentional and pleasurable activity by taking the time to present food and beverages wisely.

Adding ethnic customs to our meals can also help us appreciate the small things in life more fully. By introducing us to new flavors and cooking methods, discovering cuisines from around the world allows us to expand our culinary horizons. Cooking classic Italian pasta, creating sushi in Japan, or baking French pastries are just a few examples of how interacting with diverse culinary traditions can be enjoyable and enlightening.

Another critical component of indulging in simple pleasures is the social aspect of food and drink. A sense of community and belonging is fostered by eating meals with loved ones, friends, and even complete strangers. Potlucks, family-style dinners, and picnics are examples of communal dining events that promote camaraderie, laughing, and conversation. Sharing a meal can improve bonds between people and produce enduring memories.

In summary, savoring small pleasures in food and drink is a habit that can significantly improve our quality of life. We may develop mindfulness, appreciation, and a stronger bond with the sensory experiences our meals offer by concentrating on the intrinsic joy of eating and drinking. This method helps us to find comfort and consistency in the routines of cooking and eating, to enjoy the quality and inherent flavors of ingredients, and to savor the present moment. Joy and contentment can be brought to our everyday lives, community building, and overall well-being through the simple pleasures of food and drink, whether through modern adaptations, traditional customs, or cultural research.

CHAPTER V

Hygge in Relationships

The role of Hygge in strengthening relationships

The Danish word "hygge," which means "coziness" in English, refers to a way of thinking that values coziness, warmth, and a general sense of well-being. Hygge can be felt on its own, but its capacity to fortify bonds with others makes it very potent. This paper investigates the history, fundamental ideas, and ways in which hygge behaviors might improve relationships with others. We will comprehend how the concept of hygge promotes more meaningful and profound connections by exploring the cultural significance of this notion, as well as its psychological advantages and valuable uses.

Denmark, a nation that is usually named among the happiest in the world, is where Hygge is originating. The word comes from a Norwegian word that means "well-being," but in Denmark, it has expanded to mean providing a welcoming and comfortable environment. Hygge is not just about being comfortable on a physical level; it's also about developing a happy emotional and mental state. The concept of community and togetherness is fundamental to this philosophy, which makes hygiene a powerful tool for fostering stronger bonds between people.

Hygge is fundamentally about establishing peaceful, uncomplicated times, frequently via shared experiences. Having dinner with friends and family, sipping tea by the fire, or spending a calm evening reading with a loved one can all be simple examples of this. The focus is on savoring the present moment and avoiding the distractions of contemporary living. Hygge prioritizes these shared experiences, which helps to create the closeness and connection that are necessary for healthy partnerships.

It is impossible to exaggerate the importance of hygiene in Danish culture. It is profoundly ingrained in social conventions and practices, and it permeates daily existence. Hygge is a concept that is typically included in Danish home design, which provides for warm lighting, soft furniture, and communal areas. Hygge is a way of looking at social activities like eating with friends, celebrating holidays, or just hanging out. This cultural context offers a solid basis for establishing and preserving connections.

Hygge promotes spending quality time with one another, which is one of the main ways it improves relationships. In the fast-paced world of today, it is simple to lose touch with people around us. Our capacity to genuinely connect with others is frequently hampered by work, technology, and other distractions. Hygge combats this by establishing settings and customs that value community. A hygge-inspired dinner party, for instance, prioritizes enjoying delicious food and conversation above complex setups or electronic distractions. Participants' relationships are strengthened, and meaningful interactions are made possible in this environment.

Hygge's psychological advantages are crucial for fostering stronger bonds in partnerships. Hygge is a concept that promotes a well-being-oriented and stress-relieving atmosphere, which is favorable for good relationships. People are more inclined to interact positively and be present with others when they are at ease and satisfied. Being emotionally available is essential to developing closeness and trust, two things that make a relationship strong.

Hygge also fosters an awareness and feeling of thankfulness for life's small pleasures. This kind of thinking can change the way we see and relate to other people. By concentrating on our possessions instead of our shortcomings, we foster a spirit of giving and plenty. Kindness and empathy are encouraged by this mindset, and these qualities are necessary for sustaining relationships. Strong bonds and cherished memories can be formed when people share these times of thankfulness.

Hygge's emphasis on equality and inclusivity is another feature that improves relationships. Hygge get-togethers are usually unstructured and inclusive, dismantling social boundaries and promoting a feeling of community. In order to build solid, enduring connections, it is essential that everyone feels respected and included, which is achieved through inclusion. A sense of community and belonging is fostered by the hygge atmosphere, which is ideal for smaller gatherings as well as significant celebrations.

Hygge also promotes active listening, which is an essential relationship skill. Hygge enables people to interact more deeply with one another by establishing surroundings that encourage calm and presence. Active listening is not only hearing what is being said but also comprehending the intentions and feelings behind it. It develops empathy and a better understanding between people, both of which are necessary for trust-building and conflict resolution.

Practically speaking, hygiene may be used in daily life in a variety of ways to improve relationships. Making your home seem comfortable and welcoming is an excellent place to start. Warm, natural materials, cozy seats, and gentle lighting can all help achieve this. A hygge house is a haven where loved ones can congregate and unwind.

Meal sharing is an additional effective hygiene activity. Cooking and dining together is a great way to foster relationships and dialogue. A laid-back ambiance where everyone feels welcome is created by serving large, simple meals that everyone can enjoy. Making meals together can help strengthen relationships by encouraging cooperation and enjoyment of the process.

Additionally, Hygge stresses the value of being in the moment and slowing down. This can be especially helpful in a society where individuals frequently feel hurried and overburdened. Intimate moments can be created by taking the time to relax and enjoy a cup of coffee, read a book together, or just sit in quiet. These modest but deliberate actions can make a big difference in relationships.

Seasonal gatherings provide an additional chance to practice hygiene and build bonds with others. Holiday get-togethers, bonfires, and seasonal feasts are examples of traditions that give people a sense of continuity and shared history. These gatherings frequently adhere to hygge ideals, emphasizing community, thankfulness, and basic pleasures. Sharing a celebration strengthens relationships and produces enduring memories.

Hygge not only improves interpersonal relationships but also ties throughout the community. Hygge can be applied to social gatherings, neighborhood activities, and group projects. This kind of activity can contribute to the development of more robust and encouraging networks by creating a sense of community and belonging. Applying hygge ideas to events like book clubs, local festivals, and potlucks can make them more enjoyable for all those attending.

Another place where hygiene might help to improve connections is the workplace. Establishing a hygge-inspired workspace can boost productivity, lower stress levels, and encourage teamwork. Adding cozy seating places, promoting networking breaks, and organizing team-building events are little but effective ways to foster a sense of unity and connection. Organizations can develop more robust and cohesive teams by putting employees' well-being first and cultivating a positive work environment.

Hygge in relationships faces both possibilities and challenges in the digital age. Although technology can occasionally act as a barrier to real connection, when utilized thoughtfully, it can also strengthen connections. Hygge can be applied to virtual get-togethers, online book clubs, and video chats with loved ones. We can utilize technology to build, not destroy, our relationships by emphasizing the quality of our interactions and designing a welcoming, friendly digital environment.

Research on the benefits of social connections for wellbeing also bolsters the function of hygiene in enhancing relationships. Strong social bonds have been related in studies to improved physical and mental health, longer lifespans, and higher levels of happiness overall. These results are closely aligned with Hygge, which emphasizes emotional wellbeing and connection. Hygge can help create settings and habits that encourage happiness and connection, which can lead to happier, healthier relationships.

Furthermore, there is no one culture or way of life that hygge is exclusive to. Despite having Danish roots, the essential ideas of hygiene are universal and adaptable to a wide range of cultural settings. The emphasis on coziness, presence, and unity strikes a chord with individuals everywhere. Hygge is a lifestyle habit that can improve relationships and create a sense of community in both calm and busy villages.

To sum up, hygiene is a practical idea that can significantly improve relationships. Hygge is a concept that emphasizes coziness, presence, and togetherness. This promotes solid bonds and a happy emotional environment. Kindness, empathy, and active listening are all encouraged by its tenets of inclusivity, thankfulness, and simplicity—qualities that are crucial for wholesome relationships. Whether it be through shared meals, home settings, or neighborhood events, hygiene may be incorporated into daily life to improve our well-being and interpersonal relationships. Hygge is a lifestyle habit that promotes more vital, more meaningful relationships and a higher sense of contentment in a society where people frequently feel stressed out and isolated.

Creating shared experiences and memories

A crucial part of human life that significantly affects our sense of connection and wellbeing is the creation of shared experiences and memories. Relationships are built on these experiences and memories, which strengthen links within families, communities, and people. They give us continuity and a sense of belonging while also influencing our values and shaping our identities. This section examines the value of shared memories and experiences, how they affect relationships, the function of rituals and traditions, the impact of contemporary technology, and doable strategies for fostering these moments in day-to-day living. Shared memories and experiences are essential because they help individuals feel united and connected to one another. People develop mutual understanding, shared interests, and common ground when they participate in activities together. The sense of belonging that is fostered by this commonality is crucial for establishing and preserving solid connections. Experiences that are shared might vary from commonplace tasks like preparing meals together to unique adventures like visiting a new place. No matter how big or small, these encounters help people develop recollections that strengthen their relationships with one another.

Psychologically, developing relationships requires sharing experiences. Social psychologists claim that participating in activities together can improve emotional attachments and boost interpersonal attraction. This is so because good relationships are built on cooperation, communication, and mutual support—all of which are facilitated by shared experiences. In addition, these activities give people a chance to communicate their ideas and emotions, show off their personalities, and get to know one another better. Emotional connection and a deeper understanding are essential for the development and upkeep of solid relationships.

Family ties are formed in large part through shared experiences. A sense of continuity and stability is created by family rituals and traditions, such as weekly meals, family vacations, and holiday festivities. These times spent together offer a framework that promotes identity and family connection. They provide family members the chance to interact, talk, and make priceless memories. Intense rituals and traditions are associated with higher levels of contentment, cohesion, and adaptation in families, according to research. Family members feel more bonded to one another and to their shared past thanks to these everyday experiences.

Memory and shared experiences are equally significant in communities. Festivals, parades, and open celebrations are examples of community events that help to build a sense of community and togetherness. These gathering places give people the chance to bond over their shared culture and make memories as a group. In addition to being crucial for social cohesiveness, this sense of community can build a more robust and resilient civilization. In a community setting, shared experiences also foster social capital or the networks of trust and relationships that make societies run smoothly.

Rituals and traditions play a significant part in fostering memories and shared experiences. It can be comfortable and pleasant to have a sense of consistency and order from rituals and customs. They give life a rhythm that makes it easier for people to deal with the challenges they face every day. Anxiety and excitement are generated, for instance, by yearly holiday customs like decorating a Christmas tree or lighting Hanukkah candles. These customs help people feel a connection to their cultural heritage and family history because they are frequently passed down through the generations.

Furthermore, customs and rituals can be used to convey and uphold beliefs. For instance, Thanksgiving is a time for family get-togethers and reflection on the value of charity and community in the United States, as well as an opportunity to express appreciation. Comparably, significant historical occurrences, religious convictions, and societal ideals are frequently honored during cultural festivals across the globe. People strengthen their bonds to these ideals and to one another by taking part in these rites and customs.

Technology has changed how we create and share memories and experiences in the modern day. Thanks to digital photography, social networking, and websites that share videos, sharing memories with others is now simpler than ever. With the use of these technologies, people can keep in touch with friends and relatives who live far away, record their lives, and share their experiences with a larger audience. However, even while technology has numerous advantages, it also has drawbacks. The quality of shared experiences can occasionally be diminished by the continual presence of digital gadgets because people may be more concerned with taking pictures than with altogether participating in them. As a result, it's critical to find a balance between utilizing technology to improve shared experiences and making sure it doesn't take away from the present.

Technology can be an effective instrument for creating memories and shared experiences despite its drawbacks. Technologies like virtual reality (VR) and augmented reality (AR), for instance, provide new avenues for experiencing and sharing moments. Virtual reality (VR) has the ability to take people to new settings and eras, enabling them to enjoy immersive shared experiences even when they are in distant places. AR can improve in-person experiences by incorporating interactive features that increase their memorability and engagement. These technologies have the capacity to produce hitherto unthinkable new kinds of shared experiences.

Intentionality and effort are necessary to create shared experiences and memories in daily life. It entails scheduling time for deep conversations and communally uplifting pursuits. Sharing interests and pastimes is one approach to fostering shared experiences. Participating in activities that both people enjoy, such as cooking, gardening, hiking, or sports, can foster relationships and provide possibilities for enjoyment. These pursuits give people something in common to bond over and make enduring memories of.

Exploration and travel are two more ways to generate shared experiences. There are prospects for adventure and discovery when traveling together, whether it is to a new place or another country. It enables people to break away from their daily routines, discover foreign cultures, and make lifelong memories with one another. There are many chances for shared experiences even on short local outings, including going to a concert, museum, or neighboring park.

Another crucial component of forging memories and shared experiences is celebrating successes and landmarks. Events like graduations, anniversaries, and birthdays provide a chance to get together, celebrate, and make lifelong memories. These festivities frequently include customs and rituals that strengthen the bonds between people and give them a sense of continuity and belonging.

Being totally present and involved at the moment is another requirement for creating shared experiences. This entails putting electronics and work aside in order to concentrate on the current interaction. Critical elements of meaningful shared experiences include open communication, a genuine interest in the other person's views and feelings, and active listening. People can make more meaningful memories and stronger connections by paying attention and being present.

Besides deliberate actions, unplanned encounters can add to memories and shared experiences. The most memorable events don't always have to be orchestrated; they can sometimes come from ordinary encounters. Relationship-building experiences like an unplanned road trip, an unplanned dance party in the living room, or an evening discussion outside under the stars can forge lasting memories. Unexpected and important shared moments can arise when one embraces spontaneity and has an open mind to new experiences.

Coping with obstacles and adversity also heavily relies on shared experiences and memories. Experiencing challenging moments together, like getting through a health crisis, grieving the loss of a loved one, or going through a significant life change, can fortify bonds and foster a feeling of community. These shared experiences can strengthen resilience and serve as a consoling and supporting force. People can improve their relationships and develop a sense of common purpose and resolve by overcoming obstacles together.

Shared memories and experiences are crucial for fostering a sense of teamwork and organizational culture in the workplace. Colleagues can interact, develop trust, and make memories together through team-building exercises, retreats, and cooperative projects. These encounters can improve communication, cooperation, and job satisfaction. A positive workplace culture that is based on shared experiences and beliefs can boost productivity and employee engagement.

In educational environments, shared experiences and memories are equally important. Students can interact with their friends and make memories through extracurricular activities, group projects, and collaborative learning experiences. These encounters support a student's feeling of belonging and community in the classroom. Additionally, they foster social and emotional growth by teaching students how to collaborate, speak clearly, and form wholesome bonds with one another.

The idea of "place attachment," or the emotional connection people have to particular places, is likewise heavily reliant on shared memories and experiences. Locations that hold special memories for you, like your childhood home, a beloved vacation site, or your neighborhood community center, take on new significance and sentimentality. These locations support a sense of identification and belonging by acting as anchors for shared memories. Going back to these locations can arouse strong feelings and strengthen relationships between people.

In summary, sharing memories and experiences with others is an essential part of life and has a profound impact on our sense of wellbeing and connectedness. Relationships are built on these experiences and memories, which strengthen links within families, communities, and people. They give us continuity and a sense of belonging while also influencing our values and shaping our identities. We can create shared experiences that improve our relationships and enrich our lives by using technology, intentional activities, rituals and traditions, and unplanned moments. The formation of shared experiences and memories provides a route to more meaningful relationships and a stronger feeling of community in a world where people frequently feel alone and fragmented.

The importance of presence and active listening

It is impossible to exaggerate the value of presence and attentive listening in our daily encounters. It takes these essential communication skills to establish and preserve good relationships in both your personal and professional life. While active listening necessitates comprehending the motivations and emotions behind the words said, presence is giving your whole attention to the present. When combined, these abilities promote stronger bonds, increase empathy, and better communication in general. The importance of presence and active listening, their effects on relationships, the difficulties in putting these skills into practice, and methods for enhancing them are all covered in this section.

The basis of meaningful interactions is presence. It entails focusing solely on the person you are with, without any outside distractions. Being mindful in a society where distractions abound, including social media, cell phones, and multitasking, can be difficult. However, authentic communication requires it. We can demonstrate to people our regard and value for them by being present. This increases mutual trust and fortifies ties between people. Additionally, being present enables us to fully enjoy the moment, which improves our interactions and makes us feel more fulfilled and satisfied.

Being present requires more than just hearing what is being said; active listening is a crucial element of presence. It entails comprehending the speaker's intentions, feelings, and message. It's essential to be aware of both verbal and nonverbal signs when actively listening, including body language, tone of voice, and facial expressions. This degree of participation shows empathy and promotes rapport-building. In addition to asking questions, giving comments, and considering what has been said, active listening also entails reflection. Effective communication depends on the speaker feeling heard and understood, which is ensured by doing this.

Active listening and being present have a significant positive relationship influence. These abilities foster emotional closeness and intimacy in interpersonal relationships. People are more inclined to open up and share their views and feelings when they feel heard and understood. This improves the emotional connection between people and sparks richer, more meaningful talks. To preserve intimacy and settle disputes in love relationships, one must be there and actively listen. Partners who genuinely listen to one another are better able to comprehend one another's needs and viewpoints, which promotes more efficient problem-solving and a stronger bond.

Both being present and actively listening are crucial in family connections. When parents use these techniques with their kids, a caring and encouraging environment is created. Children are more likely to develop good communication skills and a positive self-image when they feel heard and understood. Effective parenting is facilitated by parents' increased understanding of their children's needs and emotions, which is attained through presence and active listening. These abilities improve respect and understanding between siblings, which lessens conflict and fortifies the bond between them.

Being present and actively listening are essential for teamwork and effective leadership in work environments. By putting these abilities into practice, leaders may make better decisions and boost morale by having a deeper understanding of the wants and requirements of their team members. In addition to fostering a healthy work atmosphere, active listening aids leaders in developing rapport and trust with their team. Active listening and being present are crucial for productive teamwork and problem-solving. Team members can better grasp diverse viewpoints and come up with more creative solutions and a stronger sense of camaraderie when they genuinely listen to one another.

It can be challenging to practice presence and active listening despite their value. The constant onslaught of diversions in our daily lives is one of the biggest challenges. Being really present might be challenging with the demands of work and family, social media, and smartphones. Furthermore, our own feelings and ideas can divert us from paying attention to the present moment. The propensity to listen with the goal of responding rather than understanding is another difficulty. This may result in misconceptions and inattentive listening.

It is imperative to cultivate mindfulness in order to enhance both presence and active listening. Being mindful entails seeing the current moment objectively. We can lessen the influence of distractions by training our thoughts to focus on the present moment through mindfulness practices. Practices like meditation, deep breathing, and mindful movement can help develop mindfulness. These techniques aid in mental relaxation and improve our capacity for presence in social situations.

Creating an environment that is conducive is another way to enhance presence and active listening. This entails clearing the area so that you can concentrate entirely on the conversation and reducing outside distractions. This could be putting your phone away, shutting off the TV, or looking for a private space to speak. It also entails being conscious of your own mental and physical conditions. It is hard to be present when you are worn out, anxious, or distracted. You can participate more completely in your interactions if you take care of your personal well-being.

Facilitating active listening also requires developing empathy. Empathy is the capacity to comprehend and experience another person's emotions. You can gain a deeper understanding of the speaker's viewpoint and feelings by placing yourself in their position. This improves your capacity for attentive listening and deliberate response. By acting with kindness and compassion toward others and putting in the effort to comprehend their thoughts and emotions, one can develop empathy.

Giving feedback is a crucial part of active listening. This includes summarizing the speaker's points, asking clarifying questions, and reflecting back on what you have heard. This demonstrates to the speaker your interest in and comprehension of their content. It also gives the speaker a chance to address any misunderstandings. Giving feedback improves the quality of the engagement by making the conversation more dynamic and participatory.

Maintaining awareness of nonverbal communication is another aspect of active listening. This includes tone of speech, facial expressions, and body language. Important information about the speaker's intentions and feelings can be inferred from nonverbal signs. You can better comprehend the speaker's point of view by observing these cues. Being conscious of your own nonverbal cues is also essential. Your degree of attention and engagement can be read from your facial expressions and body language. You can establish a more encouraging and exciting exchange by continuing to communicate with open and pleasant body language.

Being patient and allowing for silence are additional aspects of practicing presence and active listening. We frequently have a tendency to talk nonstop in our fast-paced world. However, in communication, silence may be a handy instrument. It gives the speaker time to think things through and digest their emotions. You may have a more deliberate and meaningful conversation if you are at ease with quiet.

Active listening and presence provide advantages that go beyond personal connections. Communities and society at large may benefit from these abilities as well. Being able to actively listen and be present in an environment where misunderstandings and disagreements are frequent might promote greater understanding and collaboration. People may help create communities that are more harmonious and peaceful by putting these abilities into practice.

For teaching and learning to be effective in educational environments, presence and active listening are crucial. Instructors who put these abilities into practice are better able to assess the needs of their pupils and offer more efficient assistance. In addition to improving rapport, active listening fosters a friendly and encouraging learning environment between teachers and students. Students can enhance their academic performance and learning by engaging in presence and active listening practices. Students can have a deeper comprehension of the subject matter and improve their communication skills by giving their studies their full attention and actively listening to their teachers and peers.

Being present and actively listening is essential in healthcare settings to deliver high-quality treatment. Healthcare professionals who put these abilities into practice can better comprehend the needs and concerns of their patients, which can result in more effective treatment and better patient outcomes. In addition to fostering rapport and trust with patients, active listening contributes to the development of a more encouraging and caring hospital environment. Patients' general well-being and level of satisfaction with their care can both benefit from feeling heard and understood.

Being present and actively listening is crucial in conflict resolution to arrive at solutions that both parties can agree with. By being fully present and listening actively to each party's perspective, mediators can better understand the underlying difficulties and encourage more successful communication. This may result in more cooperative and productive problem-solving as well as a higher chance of amicably settling disputes.

Many spiritual and cultural traditions also emphasize the value of being present and actively listening. For instance, being present and paying attention are critical components of many indigenous societies' communication techniques. Similarly, many spiritual traditions, such as Buddhism and mindfulness, emphasize the value of being wholly present and practicing active listening as a way to promote compassion and understanding.

The talent of presence and active listening can be strengthened and improved over time despite the obstacles. Through deliberate efforts to be totally present and actively listen, people can improve their communication abilities and create deeper, more meaningful connections. This calls for consistent practice, introspection, and a dedication to being totally present in the moment.

In summary, it is impossible to exaggerate the value of presence and attentive listening in our daily encounters. These abilities are necessary for creating and preserving wholesome connections in both the personal and professional spheres. While active listening necessitates comprehending the speaker's message, feelings, and intentions, presence entails giving your whole attention to the present moment. When combined, these abilities promote stronger bonds, increase empathy, and better communication in general. The talent of presence and active listening can be strengthened and improved over time despite the obstacles. Through deliberate efforts to be totally present and actively listen, people can improve their communication abilities and create deeper, more meaningful connections. Active listening and presence practices provide a technique to communicate more deeply and harmoniously in a world entire of miscommunications and distractions.

CHAPTER VI

Hygge at Work

Designing a cozy and productive work environment

Creating a comfortable and practical work environment is crucial to raising employee satisfaction, productivity, and well-being. The modern workplace has developed into an atmosphere that has a substantial impact on employees' mental and emotional well-being, going beyond simply being a physical location where duties are accomplished. A well-planned workspace can boost creativity, lower stress levels, and increase output all around. This section examines the many components of a comfortable and practical work environment, such as design, lighting, ergonomics, color schemes, and the incorporation of technology, nature, and company culture.

One of the most critical aspects of setting up a workspace for productivity is its arrangement. A well-designed layout should facilitate effortless mobility and streamlined processes. Because they make it easier to collaborate and communicate, open-plan offices are becoming more and more common. However, it's crucial to strike a balance between locations for seclusion and concentrated work and openness. Private pods or quiet rooms are valuable additions to open spaces, providing areas for staff to withdraw for focused work or private discussions. Functionality and comfort can also be improved by designating distinct zones for specific tasks, such as study rooms, individual workstations, and rest places. In addition to enhancing productivity, a thoughtful layout also promotes serenity and order.

When creating a comfortable and practical work environment, lighting is still another important consideration. The best lighting is natural light because it has been demonstrated to elevate mood, increase vitality, and enhance general wellbeing. The presence of large windows, skylights, and open areas that let natural light in can have a significant impact. If there isn't enough natural light available, you can utilize high-quality artificial lighting that looks like it. Desk lamps and dimmable overhead lights are examples of adjustable lighting choices that give employees the flexibility to customize their lighting setup to suit their needs and the tasks at hand. An environment with enough illumination is more comfortable and conducive to productivity by lowering eye strain and fatigue.

Having a comfortable and productive work environment is mainly dependent on ergonomics. Adjustable chairs, sit-stand workstations, and supportive accessories are examples of ergonomic furniture that help reduce the risk of physical pain and injuries brought on by extended sitting or bad posture. A variety of postures and motions should be supported by workstation design throughout the day. This enhances energy and focus while also promoting physical wellness. Offering workers the resources and training they need to arrange their workstations ergonomically can result in a more relaxed and effective working environment.

Color schemes have a significant impact on how a workstation feels psychologically. Colors have an effect on creativity, energy, and mood. Warm hues like orange, yellow, and red can elicit vigor and vitality, which makes them appropriate for locations where people collaborate. Because they offer a relaxing impact, cooler hues like blue and green are perfect for concentrated offices. White, gray, and beige are examples of neutral colors that can convey professionalism and balance. A vibrant and aesthetically pleasing atmosphere that accommodates a range of activities and emotions can be created in the office by strategically using color. You can utilize furnishings, artwork, and accent walls to add color without overpowering the room.

A work atmosphere can feel cozier and more inviting by including personal touches. Employee comfort and a sense of ownership can be increased by letting them add pictures, plants, and sentimental objects to their workstations. Customization helps employees feel like they belong and can create a cozier, less clinical atmosphere in the workplace. Furthermore, furnishing common areas with cozy chairs, novels, and games can promote unwinding and interpersonal communication, thereby enhancing the atmosphere at work.

It has been demonstrated that incorporating nature into the workplace, or "biophilic design," has several positive effects on both productivity and well-being. Natural materials, plants, and scenic views can all help lower stress levels, increase the quality of the air, and improve cognitive performance. Green walls, indoor plants, and water features may infuse an office with a feeling of peace and harmony with nature. Employees can take breaks and refuel in a natural environment when they have access to outdoor areas like gardens or terraces. A more comfortable and wholesome atmosphere can be produced by designing the workspace with natural components.

The modern workplace is not complete without technology, and efficiency depends on its careful integration. High-speed internet, dependable communication tools, and cutting-edge software can improve productivity and teamwork. However, in order to prevent clutter and distractions, technology should be smoothly integrated into workspace architecture. Innovative office solutions, cable management systems, and wireless charging stations can all contribute to the upkeep of a tidy and orderly workspace. Furthermore, allowing workers to use their computers and mobile devices to work remotely or in different parts of the workplace can boost output and improve job satisfaction.

The work culture of an organization is also critical in determining its characteristics. A culture that prioritizes work-life balance, open communication, and employee well-being fosters an excellent and effective environment. Policies that facilitate remote work, flexible scheduling, and regular breaks can lower burnout and increase worker satisfaction. A culture that values cooperation, acknowledgment, and ongoing education promotes participation and a feeling of community. Employee motivation and productivity are more likely to be high when they feel appreciated and supported.

Furthermore, it's essential to recognize the importance of acoustics in the workplace. Stress levels and focus can be strongly impacted by noise levels. Open-plan workspaces encourage teamwork, but they can also result in more noise and distractions. Controlling noise levels can be achieved by including sound-absorbing materials like upholstered furniture, rugs, and acoustic panels. Creating quiet areas or private spaces for concentrated work and gatherings can help lessen the adverse effects of noise. A more enjoyable auditory environment can also be produced by employing soundscaping techniques, such as playing ambient music or natural noises.

Including wellness services and programs in the office can improve workers' productivity and general well-being even more. The provision of fitness centers, meditation rooms, and nutritious food alternatives on the premises fosters both physical and emotional wellness. Wellness initiatives, such as yoga courses, mindfulness training, and ergonomic seminars, give staff members the skills they need to handle stress and lead healthy lives. Employees are more likely to be engaged and productive when they feel that their well-being is encouraged.

Considering the requirements and preferences of a varied staff is another critical aspect of creating a cozy and productive work environment. Employees can select the workspace that best fits their needs and work style by having access to a range of options, including quiet rooms, collaboration spaces, and variable seating arrangements. Ensuring that the workspace is designed with inclusivity guarantees that every employee feels supported and at ease. This can involve taking accessibility factors into account, such as installing ramps, adjustable workstations, and inclusive restrooms.

It is impossible to overestimate the value of community and social engagement in the workplace. Collaborative spaces, like lounges, break areas, and shared kitchens, are designed to promote social interaction and a sense of community. Social interactions can foster creativity and problem-solving skills in addition to improving workplace culture. Frequent social gatherings, team-building exercises, and unstructured conversation chances can boost morale and solidify bonds.

Furthermore, environmental responsibility and sustainability are becoming more and more crucial factors in workplace design. A dedication to environmental stewardship is demonstrated by the adoption of sustainable practices, such as energy-efficient lighting, recycling initiatives, and the use of eco-friendly materials. A sustainable workplace improves employee wellbeing while simultaneously benefiting the environment. Sustainable design incorporates aspects such as natural light, healthy air quality, and a connection to nature, all of which promote a more productive and healthy work environment.

In summary, creating a comfortable and practical workspace requires a comprehensive strategy that takes into account a number of factors, such as arrangement, lighting, ergonomics, color schemes, unique accents, and the fusion of technology, organizational culture, and nature. Every one of these components is essential to designing an environment that promotes workers' productivity and well-being. A well-planned workspace not only improves productivity but also fosters a supportive and unified company culture. Organizations may cultivate a workforce that is more motivated, content, and productive by putting employees' needs and preferences first and fostering a supportive and engaging atmosphere.

The role of natural light and greenery

The subject of natural light and vegetation in human habitats is broad and complex, encompassing fields such as psychology, urban planning, architecture, environmental science, and health. These factors have a significant impact on productivity, mental and physical health, aesthetic quality, and ecological sustainability. This section delves into the all-encompassing effect of natural light and vegetation, elucidating their advantages, working principles, and potential uses in many settings. We can gain a deeper understanding of the significance of incorporating these natural components into our living and working environments by thoroughly examining each component.

For human health and well-being, natural light, also known as sunshine, is essential. The circadian rhythm, our internal biological clock that controls hormone synthesis, the sleep-wake cycle, and several other physiological functions, is the mechanism by which the human body is inherently connected to natural light. This cycle is synchronized by exposure to natural light, especially in the morning. This results in more excellent sleep, happier moods, and general health benefits. In today's indoor-centric society, inadequate natural light can throw off circadian cycles, leading to sadness, insomnia, and a number of other health issues. For example, seasonal affective disorder (SAD) is a form of depression that tends to arise at specific seasons of the year, most commonly during the winter, when exposure to natural light is restricted. This emphasizes how crucial it is to plan living and working areas to optimize exposure to natural light in order to promote circadian health.

Natural light is crucial for the production of Vitamin D in the skin, in addition to its influence on circadian rhythms. Since vitamin D facilitates the absorption of calcium, it is essential for keeping strong bones. In addition, it contributes to immune system performance, lowers inflammation, and guards against a number of illnesses, including osteoporosis, cardiovascular conditions, and some types of cancer. Sunlight exposure is the most effective method of increasing Vitamin D levels. However, supplements and food sources can also supply this nutrient. Thus, making sure that buildings receive enough sunlight can help reduce the chance of vitamin D deficiency and related health problems.

There are equally important psychological benefits to natural light. Studies have demonstrated the positive effects of natural light on mood, stress reduction, and general happiness. Well-lit natural light spaces frequently evoke feelings of openness and connectedness to the outside world, which helps lessen the sense of confinement and isolation that are sometimes associated with poorly lit spaces. For instance, studies have shown that workplaces with optimal natural light exposure are associated with greater job satisfaction, lower stress levels, and improved worker productivity. Lower absenteeism and turnover rates may follow from this. In the same way, more natural light in schools has been linked to improved academic achievement and fewer behavioral problems among students. These results demonstrate the broader effects of natural light on mental and emotional health.

Patient outcomes in healthcare settings can be significantly impacted by natural light. Extensive research has demonstrated that patients in rooms with lots of natural light have shorter hospital stays, less discomfort, and less pain medicine. This is partially attributable to sunlight's mood-boosting properties, which can lower stress and anxiety and accelerate recovery. Natural light is being used more and more in healthcare facility design to generate healing settings that aid in patient recovery and wellbeing.

Greenery, which includes trees, plants, and other types of vegetation, is essential for improving human habitats. Living and working environments with more greenery have been linked to a host of health advantages, such as better air quality, lower levels of stress, and increased mental clarity. Indoor air quality is enhanced by plants because they naturally filter out air contaminants, absorb carbon dioxide, and release oxygen. This can be especially helpful in cities where air pollution is a significant issue. Better respiratory health, fewer allergies, and a decrease in the occurrence of sick building syndrome—a condition marked by symptoms like headaches, lethargy, and dizziness brought on by indoor pollutants—can all result from improved air quality.

There is a significant psychological benefit from vegetation. The idea of biophilia emphasizes the benefits of engaging with natural components by positing that humans have an innate connection to the natural world. It has been demonstrated that the presence of indoor plants and greenery lowers blood pressure, lessens stress, and enhances mood. Similar effects can be elicited by looking at views of nature or even pictures of natural settings, highlighting the significant impact of greenery on psychological wellbeing. Greenery and plants in the workplace have been shown to boost creativity, improve problem-solving skills, and increase overall job happiness. Patients who have access to natural scenery or who spend time in green areas during their hospital stays typically recover more quickly and feel less pain and stress.

Additionally, greenery enhances a space's usability and aesthetic appeal. Environments that are aesthetically pleasant and encourage reflection and relaxation are enhanced by the visual interest and beauty that natural components bring. In addition to creating focal points and softening architectural lines, plants may also provide a sense of harmony and tranquility in interior spaces. Vertical plant-covered constructions known as "green walls" can turn dull areas into lively, living installations that enhance air quality and act as acoustic insulation. Urban places become more livable and appealing when they include gardens, trees, and green spaces surrounding them. These elements also offer welcoming areas for social interaction and enjoyment.

From an environmental standpoint, incorporating flora and natural light helps achieve sustainability objectives. When natural light is used, less artificial lighting is required, which lowers energy use and greenhouse gas emissions. A lower carbon footprint and significant financial savings may result from this. Energy efficiency is further improved by passive solar design techniques, which maximize the use of natural light for heating and cooling. Greenery reduces the effects of urban heat islands, enhances biodiversity, and improves air quality, all of which contribute to environmental sustainability. In addition to lowering building temperatures and energy costs, plants and green roofs can give urban wildlife habitat. These ecological advantages highlight how crucial it is to use natural features in architectural and urban development.

Natural light and vegetation play an essential role in public places and urban planning. Green infrastructure, such as parks, greenways, and tree-lined streets, provides a number of advantages to the people living in cities and communities. Having access to green areas promotes social contact, community involvement, and physical activity. In addition to providing shade and reducing the urban heat island effect—a phenomenon where urban regions experience greater temperatures than their rural surroundings—urban greenery also helps alleviate the effects of pollution. The livability and aesthetic appeal of cities can be improved and thus can improve the general quality of life for citizens through the thoughtful design of urban areas that incorporate natural light and vegetation.

Incorporating daylight and vegetation into architectural designs has ramifications for mental well-being as well, especially when it comes to mitigating the negative impacts of urbanization and contemporary living. Urban settings are frequently typified by elevated stress, noise, and pollution levels. One much-needed break from these stresses can be found in the presence of natural elements. Natural light and green areas can foster opportunities for leisure, reflection, and relaxation—all of which are critical for mental health. The goal of therapeutic landscapes, which include restorative parks in metropolitan areas and healing gardens in hospitals, is to encourage well-being and recovery via engagement with nature. These areas show how natural light and vegetation can be therapeutically used to address mental health issues.

Adding greenery and natural light to classroom environments can improve student wellbeing and learning outcomes. It has been demonstrated that classrooms with lots of natural light and vistas of greenery enhance focus, lower stress levels, and provide a supportive learning atmosphere. Green schoolyards and outdoor classrooms offer chances for social contact, physical activity, and hands-on learning—all of which are essential components of holistic education. Academic success and kids' general development are supported in schools that place a high value on natural light and vegetation.

The advantages of natural light and vegetation in the context of office design also extend to organizational culture and staff retention. Businesses that make investments in attractive offices with lots of natural light and vegetation demonstrate their concern for the sustainability and well-being of their workforce. In addition to attracting top people and cultivating a positive corporate culture, this can improve the company's reputation. Workers are likely to be more motivated, loyal, and satisfied with their jobs when they work in environments that value natural light and vegetation. Consequently, this can result in increased output, creative thinking, and general corporate success.

Furthermore, the incorporation of vegetation and natural light is in line with more extensive cultural trends that promote sustainability, wellness, and biophilic design. Environments that promote health and well-being are becoming more and more sought after by people and organizations as knowledge of their relevance rises. The concept of biophilic design, which highlights the interdependence of humans and the environment, has become popular as a framework for developing environments that support resilience, sustainability, and well-being. This design methodology acknowledges the inherent worth of daylight and vegetation in augmenting human experiences and bolstering ecological well-being.

Natural light and vegetation play equal roles in residential design. A more comfortable and healthy living environment is provided by homes that are built to optimize natural light and feature greener Hygge. Natural light streams in from large windows, skylights, and open floor designs, making rooms feel airy and welcoming. Green walls, indoor plants, and outdoor gardens offer the beauty and health benefits of nature indoors. These architectural features support a feeling of peace, harmony with the natural world, and general wellbeing. Common areas, rooftop gardens, and courtyards in multi-family housing improve tenants' quality of life by offering chances for socializing and entertainment.

In hospital settings, natural light and vegetation are essential since they can have a significant impact on patient outcomes. For instance, healing gardens are intended to offer visitors, patients, and staff therapeutic advantages. These gardens provide a tranquil haven away from the medical setting, encouraging rest, lowering tension, and speeding healing. There is evidence that having access to natural light in patient rooms promotes better mood, less discomfort, and quicker recovery times. Furthermore, the presence of greenery and natural light can improve the working environment for healthcare professionals, lowering burnout and raising job satisfaction.

When it comes to urban planning, incorporating greenery and natural light is crucial to building resilient and sustainable cities. Parks, green roofs, and urban forests are examples of green infrastructure that supports biodiversity, helps control stormwater runoff, and lowers heat islands. In addition, these components raise property values, offer recreational activities, and raise urban living standards generally. In order to build healthier, more livable, and environmentally sustainable communities, urban planners and designers are realizing more and more how important it is to integrate natural features into cityscapes.

The advantages of daylight and vegetation also apply to shop spaces. Shops and malls that use these components typically draw more patrons and encourage more extended visits. The visual attraction of items is improved by natural light, which also makes colors seem more brilliant and makes for a more enjoyable shopping experience. Greenery enhances aesthetic appeal and fosters a calming ambiance. Examples of this include indoor plants and outdoor landscaping. Sales growth and improved customer satisfaction are two possible outcomes of these variables.

Natural light and vegetation are essential components of warm, inviting settings in hospitality design. Guests are given a sense of connection to the natural world by hotels and resorts that make the most of natural light and lush landscapes, which improves the stay overall. While external green spaces provide opportunities for relaxation and recreation, natural light in guest rooms creates a warm and inviting ambiance. These design components support hospitality venues' overall success and appeal.

Natural light and vegetation have apparent advantages, but they also have symbolic meaning in human culture and aesthetics. Light and the natural world have served as inspiration and objects of veneration throughout history. While nature has long been prized for its beauty, serenity, and capacity to sustain life, many civilizations have connected light with divinity, purity, and wisdom. These ageless associations can be evoked by incorporating natural light and vegetation into architecture and design, producing environments that have deeper cultural and emotional resonance.

Natural light and vegetation have a variety of roles in advancing sustainability. Natural light reduces the need for artificial lighting and climate control systems, which in turn lowers energy use and greenhouse gas emissions. Large windows, skylights, and reflective surfaces are examples of daylighting techniques that can drastically cut down on the demand for electric illumination during the day. By enhancing air quality, fostering biodiversity, and supplying natural cooling, greenery supports sustainability. Air conditioning is not as necessary when there are trees and other plants around to release oxygen, absorb carbon dioxide and other pollutants, and offer shade. Urban heat islands can be reduced, energy expenditures can be lowered, and buildings can be insulated with green walls and roofs. In addition to being good for the environment, these sustainable design techniques also make places that people can enjoy and live in healthier ways.

Reconnecting humans with nature in the built environment is the goal of biophilic design, which is further supported by the incorporation of vegetation and natural light. In order to improve well-being and productivity, biophilic design takes into account natural features and patterns, acknowledging human nature's fundamental attraction. Natural materials, organic shapes, vistas of the outdoors, natural light, and vegetation can all be included in this strategy. Biophilic design can enhance cognitive performance, lessen stress, and advance general health and pleasure by encouraging a connection to nature.

By designing rooms that encourage focus, creativity, and wellbeing, biophilic design concepts can improve the learning environment in educational settings. Natural light and greenery create a dynamic and relaxing atmosphere in the classroom that can enhance the engagement and performance of the students. Gardens and green schoolyards are examples of outdoor learning environments that provide possibilities for experiential education and discovery, promoting a stronger sense of connection to the natural world and an enhanced comprehension of ecological concepts.

Biophilic design has been shown to increase worker productivity, well-being, and pleasure in the workplace. A more enjoyable and motivating work atmosphere can be created with natural light and plants, which can lower stress and boost creativity. Prioritizing biophilic design in the workplace can help employers draw and keep top personnel, raise morale, and increase productivity. Businesses can cultivate a healthy company culture and achieve long-term success by designing places that support employees' well-being.

Natural light and vegetation play a vital role in healthcare environments. Healing settings that include these components can improve the working conditions for healthcare professionals as well as patients' rehabilitation and well-being. It has been demonstrated that having access to natural light in patient rooms can shorten hospital stays, lessen the need for pain medication, and enhance mood. Green spaces and healing gardens offer places to unwind and take a break, promoting mental and emotional wellbeing. Healthcare facilities can increase the overall experience of care and improve patient outcomes by establishing surroundings that promote healing and well-being.

The advantages of vegetation and natural light also apply to residential design. A more pleasant, healthy, and visually beautiful living environment is provided by homes that make the most of natural light and use greener H. Natural light streams in from large windows, skylights, and open floor designs, making rooms feel airy and welcoming. The beauty and health benefits of nature are brought within with indoor plants and garden areas, which also improve air quality, lower stress levels, and foster calmness. Common areas, rooftop gardens, and courtyards in multi-family housing improve tenants' quality of life by offering chances for socializing and entertainment.

In conclusion, natural light and vegetation play a broad and significant impact in human surroundings. These factors have a big impact on productivity, psychological wellness, physical health, aesthetic quality, and environmental sustainability. Natural light improves mood and productivity, boosts the synthesis of vitamin D, and controls circadian cycles. In addition to lowering stress and enhancing indoor and outdoor places with natural beauty, greenery also improves air quality. Quality of life, mental health, and sustainability are all aided by the use of natural light and vegetation in architectural and urban design. The incorporation of natural light and greenery into the built environment will continue to be important for developing environments that are lively, sustainable, and healthful as knowledge of their advantages grows.

Personalizing your workspace for comfort

The workspace of today is more than just a place to complete duties; it has developed into a customized setting that has an immediate impact on an individual's creativity, productivity, and general well-being. As remote work becomes more common, people have more control over their workstations and can customize them to suit their own tastes and requirements. It takes a combination of ergonomic design, visual attractiveness, and psychological factors to make your workstation comfortable. This section examines the many facets of designing a cozy and unique workstation, stressing the significance of technological integration, lighting, color psychology, organization, ergonomics, and personal touches.

Ergonomics is the cornerstone of any well-designed workspace. The science of creating and organizing objects for human use in a way that maximizes efficiency and minimizes risks is known as ergonomics. Ergonomics is primarily concerned with reducing discomfort and injury risk in the workplace while increasing productivity. The computer configuration, chair, desk, and peripherals like mouse and keyboard are essential elements of ergonomic design.

A thoughtfully selected desk is essential to an ergonomic workstation. When typing, your arms should be able to rest comfortably at a 90-degree angle on the desk. Additionally, there should be adequate room for all required equipment without creating clutter. By lowering the dangers connected with extended sitting, adjustable workstations that can alternate between sitting and standing positions provide further flexibility and health advantages.

Additionally significant is the chair. An ergonomic chair has height and tilt adjustments, promotes optimal posture, and gives the lower back the support it needs. Overall comfort is enhanced by elements including armrests, a swivel base, and lumbar support. Purchasing an ergonomic chair of superior quality can help avoid musculoskeletal problems, including back pain.

Another important consideration is where the computer screen is located. To avoid neck strain, the top of the monitor should be at or slightly below eye level, and to lessen eye strain, the screen should be placed around an arm's length away. Reaching the ideal height and distance can be facilitated by using an adjustable arm or monitor stand. Furthermore, using an ergonomic keyboard and mouse can reduce hand and wrist strain. Beneficial devices include split keyboards and mice that support the hand's natural position.

Beyond the actual arrangement, a comfortable workstation is greatly enhanced by organization. Stress and lower productivity can result from a disorganized workstation. Putting in place a system to handle documents, office supplies, and other items can help maintain a neat and functional workstation. Order can be preserved by using storage options including desk organizers, shelving, and filing cabinets. By keeping just necessary things close at hand, regular workstation cleaning lowers distractions and fosters a sense of control.

Another critical component to consider when customizing a workspace is lighting. An setting can be made cozier and less taxing on the eyes by using proper lighting. The most excellent option is natural light since it raises mood and vitality. You can get the most natural light exposure by placing the desk close to a window. However, glare needs to be controlled, and curtains or shades can help. Ambient and task lighting together are the best options when natural light isn't accessible. While task lighting, like that found on a desk lamp, concentrates light on particular regions where specialized work is done, ambient lighting illuminates the entire space. It's easy to establish the ideal lighting settings with adjustable lamps that have brightness and color temperature controls.

Another important aspect of personalizing a workstation is color psychology. In addition to evoking different emotional reactions, colors can have an impact on creativity and productivity. For example, blue is a color that is generally linked with calmness and attention, which makes it appropriate for work requiring concentration. Green is associated with balance and relaxation, both of which lower stress levels. Red can be overwhelming if used excessively, yet yellow is exciting and can encourage creativity and energy. An atmosphere that is more harmonious and inspiring can be produced by selecting a color scheme that complements both individual tastes and the nature of the task. By using wall paint, furniture, and accessories in these hues, you may add a personalized touch that can improve overall comfort and productivity.

An individual's workspace greatly enhances their comfort and well-being. It is possible to create a more welcoming and inspiring work environment by adding items that represent your interests and values. Plants, artwork, photos, and keepsakes can serve as visual stimulants and inspiration. In particular, plants have several advantages; they enhance the quality of the air, lower stress levels, and bring a bit of nature into the office. Making your workstation a place you love spending time can be achieved by choosing items that hold personal meaning for you. This will help you feel a feeling of ownership and attachment to the space.

Technology integration is yet another crucial component in creating a customized workstation. Given the growing dependence on digital tools, having a configuration that facilitates effective and pleasant technology use is vital. By keeping the workspace free of cord tangles, cable management systems help preserve its neat and orderly appearance. Wireless keyboards and mice clear up clutter and provide you with more freedom to arrange your workstation. A docking station can also simplify the process of connecting many devices, eliminating the headache of organizing multiple cords and ports.

The selection of technology itself may have an effect on comfort. Whether for virtual meetings or music listening, high-quality speakers or headphones can enhance the audio experience. For remote work to run smoothly, you need a fast and dependable internet connection. Purchasing high-quality hardware, such as a robust computer and sharp display, can increase output and lessen annoyance brought on by sluggish or broken gear. Additionally, ergonomic add-ons like a tablet holder or laptop stand can guarantee that these gadgets are used in a way that promotes proper posture and lessens strain.

A workspace's psychological atmosphere is just as significant as its technological and physical components. A place that supports mental health must take into account elements like seclusion, noise levels, and the capacity for pauses. Selecting a peaceful area for the workstation helps reduce outside noise and enhance concentration. Unwanted sounds can be blocked out with the use of a white noise machine or noise-canceling headphones. Having some solitude in the workstation can improve comfort and lower stress levels, particularly in shared or open-plan environments.

Having the capacity to take regular breaks is crucial for preserving both mental health and productivity. It can be beneficial to plan the workstation such that there is a place to relax and read on occasion, or even just an excellent chair for when you need to take a break from the desk. Including components that encourage rest, such as a stretching area or a meditation nook, can help enhance wellbeing. Preventing burnout and preserving an excellent work-life balance require regular scheduling of breaks and establishing boundaries between work and leisure time.

The ability to adjust a workstation to changing requirements and tastes is another element of creating a comfortable haven. The workstation should be flexible to accommodate changing job demands and personal preferences. Different interests and tastes can be accommodated with modular furniture and variable layouts. For instance, a chair with movable settings and a desk with height adjustment allow for customization to fit various jobs and body types. Having the flexibility to occasionally shift the desk can also offer new inspiration and a different viewpoint.

The comfort and individuality of a workspace can be further improved by incorporating customs and routines from home. One way to provide structure and balance in the workplace is to establish rituals that indicate the beginning and end of the workday. A sense of routine and comfort can be created by simple rituals like making a cup of coffee or tea at the desk in the morning and cleaning up the workspace at the end of the day. Making these routines unique to each person's tastes might help the office feel more like a private retreat.

Lastly, it's critical to maintain awareness of health and wellbeing in the workplace. A setting can be made more cozy and encouraging by adding components that help both mental and physical health. An exercise ball chair or a standing desk, for example, can promote mobility and enhance posture. Having wholesome snacks on hand and staying hydrated helps promote general wellbeing. Furthermore, engaging in mindfulness or relaxation exercises like meditation or deep breathing might help you focus better and feel less stressed.

Finally, incorporating personal touches, technological integration, lighting, psychology of color, organization, ergonomic design, and psychological well-being are all important aspects of creating comfortable and personalized working. Through the customization of a workspace to align with individual tastes and requirements, people can improve their general well-being, creativity, and productivity. To make sure that your office is not just helpful but also a location where you feel inspired and at ease, it's essential to find a balance between personal expression and functionality. A comfortable and customized office will become increasingly important as work continues to change, becoming a necessary component of contemporary living.

CONCLUSION

I hope that by the time you finish reading "Hygge Harmony: Embracing Coziness in Everyday Life," you will have a better knowledge of the Hygge concept and be able to apply its tenets in your day-to-day activities. Hygge is a timeless way of living that prioritizes coziness, contentment, and connection rather than just being a passing fad. Embracing Hygge can help you create a life that is full of harmony, warmth, and joy by elevating everyday moments to remarkable ones.

We have looked at the many facets of Hygge in this book, beginning with its Danish origins and cultural relevance. We explored the fundamental principles of Hygge, including coziness, mindfulness, and simplicity, and how they might improve our mental and emotional health. You've made the first move toward living a life that values true happiness and wellbeing by comprehending the principles of Hygge.

Creating a Hygge atmosphere in your house is an essential component of this concept. We talked about how to use natural materials, textures, and lighting to create rooms that encourage coziness and comfort. Your living area can be made more peaceful and conducive to rest by clearing out and simplifying things. This feeling of peace is further enhanced by bringing nature inside your house, whether it be through plants or natural décor.

There is no season or place where hygge cannot be found. We looked at ways to live hygge year-round and discovered particular chances to be cozy in every season. Hygge wants us to be happy no matter what the weather or situation, from the coziness of winter get-togethers to the excitement of summer picnics. You may sustain a year-round sense of joy and well-being by modifying your Hygge routines to fit the seasonal changes.

Hygge has the power to change ordinary tasks. You may bring warmth and contentment to activities like cooking, crafting, and even work by adopting a Hygge mindset. Hygge can be incorporated into your daily life in a variety of ways, such as through self-care routines, creative hobbies, and mindful eating and drinking. These routines serve as a helpful reminder to slow down, appreciate the present, and find joy in the little things.

Connections are the core of Hygge. A fulfilling life requires forging solid bonds with friends, family, and the community. We talked about how to build these relationships by having meaningful conversations and sharing experiences, making memories that will make you happy for a long time. Hygge highlights the value of being in the moment and developing close relationships with people around us, whether through private get-togethers or communal activities.

Integrating the tenets of Hygge into your professional life can significantly improve both your wellbeing and productivity. You may add a touch of Hygge to your work environment by making your workstation comfortable and valuable, keeping a good work-life balance, and developing strong bonds with your coworkers. This all-encompassing strategy makes sure that your employment enhances your general sense of contentment and happiness.

Being mindful and growing yourself is essential to leading a life influenced by Hygge. We talked about how important it is to have an optimistic outlook, practice appreciation, and create realistic goals. Through an emphasis on self-improvement and awareness, you may face obstacles in life with fortitude and elegance. Hygge inspires us to enjoy the process of growing and to cherish the trip.

When you travel with a Hygge mindset, you may have a laid-back and pleasurable time seeing new locations. You may design enjoyable and meaningful travel experiences by prioritizing comfort and connection when organizing your excursions. Hygge-inspired travel encourages a spirit of exploration and relaxation, whether you're traveling to new places or taking a staycation.

Another essential component of Hygge is sustainability. You can live sustainably by implementing eco-friendly habits and making moral decisions. Hygge urges us to consider how our actions affect the environment and to make decisions that will contribute to a sustainable future. Our dedication to sustainability improves our own wellbeing in addition to the environment.

It's crucial to strike a balance between technology and Hygge in the digital age. We talked about how to set tech-free zones, control screen time, and use technology thoughtfully. You can make sure that technology complements your Hygge lifestyle rather than takes away from it by learning to live in digital harmony.

As you proceed on your Hygge journey, never forget that the core of Hygge is discovering joy in connection and simplicity. Prioritize your health, treasure your relationships, and enjoy the little moments of warmth. In your pursuit of a happy and harmonious life, "Hygge Harmony: Embracing Coziness in Everyday Life" is not simply a manual but a constant friend. I hope you have many days full of coziness, warmth, and the enduring spirit of hygge.

Thank you for buying and reading/ listening to our book. If you found this book useful/ helpful please take a few minutes and leave a review on the platform where you purchased our book. Your feedback matters greatly to us.